Conceptions of and Corrections to Majoritarian Tyranny

Conceptions of and Corrections to Majoritarian Tyranny

Donald L. Beahm

LEXINGTON BOOKS
Lanham • Boulder • New York • Oxford

LEXINGTON BOOKS

Published in the United States of America
by Lexington Books
4501 Forbes Boulevard, Suite 200, Lanham, Maryland 20706

PO Box 317
Oxford
OX2 9RU, UK

British Library Cataloguing in Publication Information Available

Library of Congress Cataloging-in-Publication Data

Beahm, Donald L., 1953-
    Conceptions of and corrections to majoritarian tyranny / Donald L. Beahm.
        p. cm.
    Includes bibliographical references and index.
    ISBN 0-7391-0334-2 (cloth : alk. paper) — ISBN 0-7391-0659-7 (pbk. : alk. paper)
        1. Representative government and representation—United States. 2. Unites
States—Politics and Government. 3. Majorities. 4. Minorities—United States. I. Title.

JK 1726 .B43 2002
321.8'01—dc21

Printed in the United States of America

♾™ The paper used in this publication meets the minimum requirements of American
National Standard for Information Sciences—Permanence of Paper for Printed Library
Materials, ANSI/NISO Z39.48–1992.

For Renee, Tonya, and Jeramie

Contents

Acknowledgments

I would first of all like to thank my parents, Merle R. Beahm and Mary G. Beahm, whom without none of this would have been possible. I offer my sincerest respect to all of the veterans who served during World War II, as my Dad did, and for those who loved them and anxiously awaited their return, as my Mom did. You saved us from tyranny and are all heroes in my mind. I thank you. Our family was fortunate that our loved one returned.

I would also like to thank my sisters Linda Hultgren and Bonnie Nelson, my brother Merlin Beahm, all of my nieces, nephews, in-laws, and friends for being supportive while I finished this work. My thanks also go to the members of my Supervisory Committee: Dr. John Gruhl, Dr. John Hibbing, Dr. Benjamin Rader, and especially to Dr. Philip Dyer. All of your comments and recommendations were very helpful. Dr. Dyer acted as the main advisor on this dissertation, and its completion simply would not have been possible without him. I would also like to thank all of the people from Lexington Books for their assistance in completing this project.

Finally, my gratitude is extended to all Vietnam veterans for their service to our country.

Chapter 1

Introduction

It is of great importance in a republic not only to guard the society against the oppression of its rulers, but to guard one part of the society against the injustice of the other part.

—James Madison. *The Federalist Papers*, No. 51

The fundamental tenet of democracy is that the majority rules. This concept has filtered down through time to us in such a pervasive fashion that it has become the doctrine of democracy. This doctrine of democracy has been adopted by multifarious governments endorsing the utilitarian principle that what is best for the people is what is chosen by the majority. This main tenet of democracy is potentially flawed, because it does not adequately account for the very thing that most threatens the existence of democracy. This threat comes from majoritarian oppression. In a letter written 17 October 1788, James Madison warned Thomas Jefferson that:

Wherever the real power in a Government lies, there is the danger of oppression. In our Governments the real power lies in the majority of the Community, and the invasion of private rights is cheifly *sic* to be apprehended, not from acts of Government contrary to the sense of its constituents, but from acts in which the Government is the mere instrument of the major number of the constituents (Madison 1977, 11:298).

Madison had expressed concerns about the injustice of majoritarian oppression prior to his letter to Jefferson in *Federalist 51* (1961, 323). But Madison was not the first to express recognition of this problem. Long before Madison, Plato (1981, 47), and Aristotle (1978, 122, 134, 261) described similar views on the danger of the majority becoming overbearing. Since Madison's warning, a number of other authors have perceived threats from the majority as the most dangerous to a democracy (Tocqueville 1969, 248, 252, 260; Calhoun 1953, 22-

1

25, 35; Mill 1977, 448, 459). Oppression by the majority, in all of its various conceptions, has come to be known as the "Tyranny of the Majority."

Although the phrase "Tyranny of the Majority" is often used as though it were a singular theory that is well defined and clearly understood, it is in fact none of the aforementioned. What the tyranny of the majority is, and how to guard against it, has been the subject of a number of nebulous alternative conceptions and corrections. No single theorist has attempted to construct a comprehensive theory of the tyranny of the majority. Those who have written on the issue have done so in a mostly indirect fashion where other ends (usually political) were being pursued. The result has been a poverty of clarity on the matter (Dahl 1956, 4-33).

The limited constitutional government established in the United States at the convention in 1787 was marked by Madison's desire to prevent majoritarian oppression from dominating the new government. Although obvious contradictions to minority protections, such as slavery and continuing discrimination against racial minorities, demonstrates the failures that all too often have afflicted our system. Madison was earnest in making the concept of the tyranny of the majority a focus of concern in the fledgling days of the American republic. The phrase "Madisonian Democracy" has come to symbolize his contributions in this area. (Dahl 1956, 4) In her book *The Tyranny of the Majority*, Lani Guinier refers to a majority that rules but does not dominate as a "Madisonian Majority" (1994, 6). Thus, America has a rich, original, and sometimes conflicting heritage to draw upon concerning protection of the few from a domineering majority. Not unimportant is the fact that America had Madison to set the agenda.

Historical Examples of Tyranny of the Majority

Regardless of Madison's attempt to establish protections against the tyranny of the majority, examples of it have flourished over the last 210 years. Two of the most recognized examples of majoritarian tyranny in the history of the United States are the Civil War and discrimination against racial minorities (Roper 1989, 87; Guinier 1994, 103). These two examples provide a provocative paradox for analysis of the issue, because they both had to deal with discrimination against a racial minority that resulted in decidedly different outcomes. In the case of the Civil War a tyrannizing majority (the North) forced abolition on the South. While one certainly could suggest that this was a moral exercise in majority will, it was nevertheless seen by Southerners at the time as an act of a tyrannical majority. The result of the outcome of the Civil War was to end one abominable form of discrimination, slavery, only to have the specter of various other manifestations raised. Discrimination against racial minorities continued virtually unabated for many years, and it continues today in the areas of employment, housing, education, and voting (Guinier 1994), leaving American history rife with ugly examples of what the injustice of majoritarian oppression can do.

Other examples of tyranny of the majority in the United States have been related to the treatment of communists and socialists. In the period from 1919 till 1927 the Supreme Court upheld the convictions of communists and socialists accused of violating the Espionage Act of 1917, the Sedition Act of 1918, and other state laws that were intended to limit their speech. The Court determined that their speech was a "clear and present danger" to the government, when, in fact, their speech provoked little apprehended threat (*Schenk v. United States; Frohwerk v. United States; Debs v. United States; Abrams v. United States; Gitlow v. New York; Whitney v. California*).

In the case of *Dennis v. United States* (1951) the speech of communists was once again limited when members of the American Communist party were convicted of violating the Smith Act of 1940. The 1950s were a period in which tensions between the United States and the Soviet Union had risen dramatically. The Cold War had erupted signifying those tensions and Senator Joseph McCarthy (R-Wis.) exploited the situation, charging various government officials with being communists, despite the fact that he had almost no substantive evidence to back up his claims. These "witch-hunts" came to be referred to as McCarthyism. This remains one of the clearer examples in the United States of majoritarian tyranny being exercised by misuse of public institutions, stimulated by public opinion. McCarthy, by way of demagoguery, had managed to sweep the country into a paranoid frenzy against suspected communists that influenced court decisions and damaged innocent people (Fried, 1997).

Senator McCarthy was later discredited and the Supreme Court began to demonstrate greater tolerance toward the First Amendment free expression rights of communists by the late 1950s and early 1960s (*Yates v. United States; Scales v. United States*). However, the damage had already been done to many individuals. Madison's corrections to the tyranny of the majority implanted in the Constitution (checks and balances), along with his belief that factions would cancel each other out for the most part (Madison 1961, 77-84), had not been adequate to prevent these violations from occurring, even though they may have played a part in remedying later comparable situations.

A similar failure of Madisonian corrections to work before tyrannical majoritarianism could do its damage resulted in religion being used to tyrannize those with minority points of view. Organized prayer and Bible readings occurred in many public schools throughout the country prior to 1962. The prayers were voluntary and children who were not followers of the Christian faith could leave the room if they did not want to participate in those organized religious activities. The Supreme Court in 1962 and 1963 finally determined that these religious activities were probably not as voluntary as they were portrayed, because leaving the room is often seen as punishment for children. Therefore, the Court ruled that these rituals violated the establishment clause of the First Amendment (*Engle v. Vitale; Abington School District v. Schempp*).

Religious activities continue to pervade public institutions in the United States. Prayers are recited in many legislative assemblies and in many courtrooms at the beginning of their daily activities. These religious practices and others similar to them continue to be tolerated despite the obvious contradictions of the idea of separation of church and state. Again, the effect of public opinion in pressuring people to accept the majority point of view cannot be underestimated.

The evidence from the historical-legal record indicates that, in America, the tyranny of the majority exists as a phenomenon. The problem is that the alternative conceptions and corrections to the tyranny of the majority are not clear, and are inadequate. Although the preventative actions taken heretofore have been helpful, they have not been enough to avoid a recurring problem.

Approach

Because I find the alternative conceptions and corrections to the tyranny of the majority to be unclear and inadequate, it is my intention in this study to clarify and analyze the perspectives of five different authors on the subject. I will examine James Madison, Alexis de Tocqueville, John C. Calhoun, Robert A. Dahl, and Lani Guinier on their conceptualizations of the tyranny of the majority, their definition of tyranny, their perception of rights, and their corrections to the tyranny of the majority. If indeed the tyranny of the majority is the most egregious threat to democracy, as Madison, Tocqueville, Calhoun, and Mill have indicated, then I believe that it is necessary to be clear about what it is, how it can be defined, how rights have influenced our thinking about it, and what has been done to prevent, or correct it.

I have decided to focus on these four particular points because I regard them as being the most important elements of the tyranny of the majority. First, I will clarify and analyze the alternative conceptualizations of the tyranny of the majority, which I believe will shed light on how the five authors interpret its meaning. Second, of the five authors only Madison has provided an explicit definition of tyranny. By clarifying and analyzing each author's contribution to the definition of tyranny, I hope to arrive at a more meaningful definition of tyranny, and of tyranny of the majority. Third, I will demonstrate that how an author thinks about rights affects how he or she perceives the idea of the tyranny of the majority. Fourth, I will clarify and analyze each author's view on how to correct for the tyranny of the majority.

In the last chapter I will synthesize the perspectives of the five authors on the four elements of the tyranny of the majority. I will not be searching for a general theory of the tyranny of the majority that includes all of the major contributors to the subject. What I will be seeking is a unification of thought on the four points, derived from these particular authors who have written on the American problem. I believe this synthesis will provide more cohesiveness to the general idea of the tyranny of the majority. I will also suggest what I think can be done to prevent, or correct for, the tyranny of the majority.

Certainly other authors have something to say about the subject, and various democratic republics have suffered from similar majoritarian problems. Nevertheless, this study will be limited to works dealing with the American political system, not only because America was early and unique in establishing protection for minority points of view that may be trammeled upon by majoritarian based governments (Madison 1961, 77-84, 301, 309, 322-25), but also because America has some peculiarities, such as winner-take-all single-member districts, that few other systems have. Additionally, limiting this study to a single political system will assist in avoiding the pitfall of overgeneralizing findings. The tyranny of the majority exists in a number of different modes. With the broad diversity in the construction of political systems throughout the world, the application of the concepts formulated for one system may or may not be suitable to another. For the sake of clarity, the American political system provides a limited context in which to explore the concepts of the tyranny of the majority, while not being limited by too few contributions by theorists on the subject to be constrictive.

Even within the scope of American political thought, I will only analyze a limited number of contributors to the topic. A chapter will be devoted to Madison, Tocqueville, and Calhoun. Dahl and Guinier will be discussed jointly in the fifth chapter. Dahl has been a consistent critic of the notion of the tyranny of the majority over the last fifty years and deserves a response. Guinier will be reviewed as a modern significant contributor to the literature on the subject.

There are several reasons why Madison, Tocqueville, Calhoun, Dahl, and Guinier have been chosen for inspection and to provide the principal intellectual foundation for the foregoing investigation. First, all of these authorities have written on the subject of the tyranny of the majority as it relates to American government and politics, and they are among the foremost progenitors of the concepts of and corrections to the tyranny of the majority.

Second, all of these contributors offer broadly different views on what the tyranny of the majority is and how to correct for it. Madison interpreted the danger as coming primarily from "acts in which the government is the mere instrument of the major number of the constituents" (Madison 1977, 11:298). Hence, he saw the threat of the tyranny of the majority originating with the people, but being brought to bear through the government primarily by way of the legislature (Madison 1961, 309), since it is the branch that "predominates" (322). Madison's:

> remedy for this inconveniency is to divide the legislature into different branches; and to render them, by different modes of election and different principles of action, as little connected with each other as the nature of their common functions and their common dependence on the society will admit (Madison 1961, 322-23).

Tocqueville believes the majority is respected because everyone hopes to be a part of it at some time. The majority has "immense actual power and a power of opinion which is almost as great" (Tocqueville 1969, 248). He believes the tyranny of the majority is tempered by civic and political associations; the absence of administrative centralization; the counterbalancing effect of the American legal profession; and by the jury as a political institution (Tocqueville 1969, 262-76). Calhoun offers the most complete philosophical underpinning for his views. Rather than proposing a social contractarian point of view that respects the ideas of a state of nature and natural rights, Calhoun believes that society has always existed and that the only rights people have are those granted by society (Calhoun 1953, xvii-xix). This logic is also a thinly disguised veil for his defense of slavery. In democratic governments Calhoun considers the problem with the tyranny of the majority to be with numerical majorities as opposed to concurrent majorities. Numerical majorities regard "numbers only" and don't reflect the community interests. Concurrent majorities pay attention to "interests as well as numbers" (Calhoun 1953, 22-23).

Dahl holds a contrary view from the other authors, but not an unimportant one. He finds that at the Constitutional Convention, and in the *Federalist Papers*, there was not much concern for the tyranny of the minority. He thinks that the "Founding Fathers" were imbalanced in their distress over the legislature being dominated by the majority, at the expense of ignoring the danger of tyranny in the executive. He suggests that "internal checks," such as one's social conscience and attitudes, are more likely to prevent tyranny from arising in a society than are the checks in the government set out by Madison and other founders (Dahl 1956, 9-19).

Guinier argues that "there is nothing inherent in democracy that requires majority rule" (Guinier 1994, 17). She contends that "winner-take-all" (55, 79, 82) "single-member districts" (82-86) deny blacks "authentic representation" (55-58. See explanation of "authentic representation" on page 72 and 73), and she supports "interest representation" (117-18) through "cumulative voting" (14-16, 119, 123, 137). She states that "The fundamentally important question of political stability is how to induce losers to continue to play the game. Political stability depends on the perception that the system is fair to induce losers to continue to work within the system rather than to try to overthrow it" (Guinier 1994, 9). If any group is always excluded, systemic political solutions will be ignored, and less accepted "alternatives" will be attempted (51).

A third reason why these authors have been chosen is that there is a chronological historical development to their writings that serves to explain an evolution of thought on the subject and explores some of the diversity in approaches. Madison, being a man of both the eighteenth and nineteenth centuries, lived in a time when he had the opportunity to contribute to a government his ideas about the threat of the tyranny of the majority. He also experienced how the government he and the other founding fathers had created worked as a practical matter. Few theorists have had the experience of attempting to apply the concepts that they believed in to a government which they helped construct.

Tocqueville, a Frenchman of the nineteenth century, had a viewpoint of America and its system that was, perhaps, a bit more objective than those who lived within, or were involved in creating the system. Tocqueville cast an optimistic but cautious eye toward the development of democratic ideas in America. Certainly he was looking at America's experiment with democracy for its —broader applications in Europe, particularly in France (Tocqueville 1969, 196). Nonetheless, Tocqueville saw strengths and weakness in the American system in ways that others did not. For example, his view that lawyers would act to counterbalance the threats of the tyranny of the majority by acting as a brake, because of their "habit of advancing slowly" in matters, was not foreseen by other contributors on the subject, and may come as somewhat of a surprise to the modern reader (268-69).

Calhoun, a nineteenth-century American who felt the sting of the tyranny of the majority directly, commented on the shortcomings of the countermeasures. In his essay *A Disquisition on Government*, Calhoun proposes that some provision other than suffrage is needed in order for constitutional government to work. The "other provision" that Calhoun proposed was the use of concurrent majorities—or, what he sometimes referred to as constitutional majorities. The idea behind concurrent majorities is that, beyond suffrage, there will be a governmental apparatus by which the interests in society that are prone to unfair treatment by the government will have a way to concur in the government decisions, or veto it if it harms their concerns (Calhoun. 1953, 19-21). Calhoun was proposing that a new negative power be added to the Constitution along with the existing checks and balances because he believed that both negative and positive powers were necessary to a government so it could both act and resist certain actions (Calhoun 1953, 28). The negative power could be a "veto, interposition, nullification, check, or balance of power" (28). Concurrent majorities are necessary in Calhoun's view, because without them numerical majorities would lead eventually to absolute government (28).

Dahl, a twentieth-century white male, has observed both the failure of prevention and attempts at correction to the tyranny of the majority, but has taken the view that democratic processes are the cure to the problem of the minority being denied its political rights. He does not believe that the majority may "rightly use its primary political rights to deprive a minority of its primary political rights" (Dahl 1989, 171). Dahl contends that if the majority would deny the minority their primary political rights, they would be affirming that they aren't able to govern by the democratic process. He supports the notion that protection of primary political rights is essential to the political culture of a stable democracy (171-72).

Guinier is a twentieth-century black female that has been a personal witness to both failures to protect minority points of view and attempts at correcting those failures. She has worked as a civil rights lawyer, where she has had direct involvement with issues related to minority protection. It is somewhat ironical that she should offer up interest representation and cumulative voting as alternative voting mechanisms, because her suggestions are not far different from the idea of concurrent majorities that Calhoun suggested. The irony is that a black woman of the 1990s is offering a similar remedy to being tyrannized by the majority as did a white male from the nineteenth-century that defended slavery. This is not to suggest that the moral justification for what they are trying to protect is equivalent, but the methods are much the same. She is supportive of a minority veto—or negative, as Calhoun would have put it. They are both favoring a form of interest representation. These authors represent a vast array of ideas about the tyranny of the majority. While they do not exhaust the subject by any means, they do provide enough variety to stimulate considerable thought about the issue. Madison initiated much of the discussion on the topic in America. He is the appropriate one to begin with. Original spellings will be maintained.

Note

Madison was attempting to garner votes for ratification of the Constitution when the *Federalist Papers* were written. Calhoun was defending slavery, and Lani Guinier was reacting to her withdrawn nomination to be assistant attorney general in charge of the Civil Rights Division.

References

Abington School District v. Schempp, 374 U.S. 203 (1963).

Abrams v. United States, 250 U.S. 616 (1919).

Aristotle. 1978. *The Politics of Aristotle*. London: Oxford University Press.

Calhoun, John C. 1953. *A Disquisition on Government and Selections on the Discourse*. New York: Liberal Arts Press.

Commager, Henry Steele. 1993. *Commager on Tocqueville*. Columbia: University of Missouri Press.

Dahl, Robert A. 1956. *A Preface to Democratic Theory*. Chicago: University of Chicago Press.

————. 1989. *Democracy and Its Critics*. New Haven, Conn.: Yale University Press.

Debs v. United States, 249 U.S. 211 (1919).

Dennis v. United States, 341 U.S. 494 (1951).

Engle v. Vitale, 370 U.S. 421 (1962).

Frohwerk v. United States, 249 U.S. 204 (1919).

Fried, Albert. 1997. *McCarthyism: The Great American Red Scare. A Documentary History*. Ed. Albert Fried. New York: Oxford University Press.

Gitlow v. New York, 268 U.S. 652 (1925).

Guinier, Lani. 1994. *The Tyranny of the Majority: Fundamental Fairness in Representative Democracy*. Foreword by Stephen L. Carter. New York: Free Press.

Madison, James, Alexander Hamilton, and John Jay. 1961. *The Federalist Papers*. Intro. Clinton Rossiter. NewYork: New American Library.

Madison, James. 1977. *The Papers of James Madison*. Vol. 11. *1788-1789*. Ed. Robert A. Rutland, Charles F. Hobson, William M. E. Rachal, and Jeanne K. Sisson. Charlottesville: University Press of Virginia.

Mill, John Stuart. 1977. *Considerations on Representative Government. Collected Works*. Vol. XIX. *Essays on Politics and Society*. Ed. by J. M. Robson. Introduction by Alexander Brady. University of Toronto Press.

Plato. 1981. *Five Dialogues: Euthyphro, Apology, Crito, Meno, Phaedo*. Trans. G. M. A. Grube. Foreward by Donald J. Zeyl. Indianapolis: Hackett Publishing.

Roper, Jon. 1989. *Democracy and Its Critics: Anglo-American Democratic Thought in the Nineteenth Century*. London: Unwin Hyman.

Safford, John L. 1995. "John C. Calhoun, Lani Guinier, and Minority Rights." *PS* 26 (2): 211-16.

Scales v. United States, 367 U.S. 203 (1961).

Schenk v. United States, 249 U.S. 47 (1919).

Spain, August O. 1951. *The Political Theory of John C. Calhoun*. New York: Bookman Associates.

de Tocqueville, Alexis. 1969. *Democracy in America*. Trans. George Lawrence. Ed. J. P. Mayer. New York: Harper and Row.

Whitney v. California, 274 U.S. 357 (1927).

Yates v. United States, 354 U.S. 298 (1957).

Chapter 2

Madison

James Madison once replied to an admirer who had referred to him as "the father of the Constitution," "You give me to which I have no claim, in calling me 'the writer of the Constitution of the United States.' This was not, like the fabled Goddess of Wisdom, the offspring of a single brain. It ought to be regarded as the work of many heads & many hands" (Madison 1966, xi-xii).

Indeed many others made significant contributions to the Constitutional Convention, but Madison's preparation and sustained efforts demonstrate he is worthy of the title (Madison 1966, xii-xiii). He should be remembered as both a great statesman and an important political thinker. It is as a political theorist that I consult him now (Madison 1953, 1-21).

On the subject of the tyranny of the majority, Madison's insight cannot be overlooked. He set the foundation for further examination of the subject by Tocqueville, Calhoun, Dahl, and Guinier. His explanations of how majority factions can come to dominate the government are key to comprehending the threat they may pose. His conceptions on how to correct for majoritarian tyranny still operate by way of the Constitution today.

Madison's Tyranny of the Majority

There are several criteria to consider when examining Madison's view of how the tyranny of the majority takes root and can negatively affect a democratic republic. Madison's emphasis is on how social causes influence the political process of democracy, causing it to produce majority tyranny. Madison recognizes that the tyranny of the majority originates from the people themselves (Madison 1977, 11:298). There is the necessary connection between the people and their representatives within the government (suffrage), and this relationship can produce tyranny by a domineering faction compelling the government to act in its behalf at the expense of minority groups.

Madison also sees tyranny as a threat within the government, predominantly within the legislature (Madison 1961, 51:322; Dahl 1956, 21-22). A majority of the legislators can exercise a tyrannical power over the minority by refusing to acknowledge their concerns, but the danger is not limited to that branch alone. The president and the judiciary can create their own forms of tyranny by being pressured from the outside by citizens insisting on having their way, or by members within branches making decisions or implementing policies that are tyrannical in nature. These decisions or policies could tyrannize a minority or a majority.

Central to Madison's foreboding about tyranny in a democratic republic is the debilitating power that factions can have on popular government. Since tyranny of the majority stems from the people and their desire to organize into groups to lobby for their interests, something must be done to mitigate majorities and their overbearing influence. Madison understands that "the causes of faction cannot be removed" (Madison 1961, 10:80). Nevertheless, the causes of faction can be controlled by the republican principle of majority rule when the faction is a minority. In other words, the people squelch the problem of tyranny of the minority by voting it down. The real problem surfaces when the faction is a majority that wields its power without regard to the minority. Madison recognizes that in a society the size of the United States there will be so many interests and classes that the chance of a majority faction usurping too much power is small. However, when this happens the result is unwelcome. Madison declares that "measures are too often decided, not according to the rules of justice and the rights of the minor party, but by the superior force of an interested and overbearing majority" (Madison 1961, 10:77).

He continues by stating, "When a majority is included in a faction, the form of popular government, on the other hand, enables it to sacrifice to its ruling passion or interest both the public good and the rights of other citizens" (Madison 1961, 10:80).

The issue then becomes how to deal effectively with majority factions so that they do not predominate within the government itself. As Madison proposes, "Relief is only to be sought in the means of controlling its effects" (Madison 1961, 10:80).

The rights of citizens who are not in the majorities come under the greatest risk of tyranny in a democratic republic. This tyranny is different from others, and yet there are similarities in all types of tyranny. A definition of tyranny of the majority is necessary to gain a firmer grasp of its meaning. Madison provides such a definition, but the clarity of his meaning leaves something to be desired.

Madison's Addition to the Definition of Tyranny

Madison defines tyranny in this way:

> The accumulation of all powers, legislative, executive, and judiciary, in the same hands, whether of one, a few, or many, and whether hereditary, self-appointed, or elective, may justly be pronounced the very definition of tyranny (Madison 1961, *Federalist 47*:301).

Dahl interprets Madison's explicit definition of tyranny to mean that "tyranny is every severe deprivation of a natural right" (1956, 6). Dahl derives his interpretation of Madison's definition from the idea that what Madison was attempting to say was that "The accumulation of all powers in the same hands would lead to severe deprivations of natural rights and hence to tyranny" (Dahl 1956, 6).

Dahl's reconstruction of Madison's explicit definition that "tyranny is every severe deprivation of a natural right" (1956, 6), appears to be accurate. Throughout *Federalist 47* the thrust of Madison's case is that for any one branch to have all of the power, or if a government is limited to one source of power (such as a monarchy, an aristocratic ruling elite, or a democracy that has only a legislature, for example) is not only to invite tyranny, but in Madison's view, is tyranny. *Ergo*, an absence of separation of powers is tyranny. The problems that Dahl has with his derivation of Madison's definition is that it is "unnecessarily arbitrary and argumentative" because "natural rights" and "severe deprivation" are not specified clearly enough (Dahl 1956, 6-7).

Later, in *A Preface to Democratic Theory*, Dahl states that "it is self-evident that the definition of tyranny would be entirely empty unless natural rights could somehow be defined" (Dahl 1956, 23). Rossiter (1953, 362-363) concurs with Dahl that there was not specific individual agreement among revolutionary period political theorists on which "rights" are "natural rights" (Dahl 1956, 7), but, as he later acknowledges in *The Political Thought of the American Revolution*, there was something akin to an "American consensus" on what those rights are (Rossiter 1963, chap. 4). This consensus can be found in The Declaration of Independence.

The failure on the part of Madison to define what was envisioned by natural rights left Dahl concluding that Madison's intended definition of tyranny was incomplete, and that rendered the concept of the tyranny of the majority inert. I disagree. Since there was an "American Consensus" on what natural rights were (Rossiter 1963, chap. 4), the notion of natural rights was generally understood. As I will discuss in the next section, I believe that Madison didn't define natural rights clearly because he understood that it was up to the people to determine which rights were natural to them (Morgan 1988, 131-59; Declaration of Independence). If we include my contention that the people determine what their natural rights are, then the reconstructed definition of tyranny according to

Madison, Dahl, and Beahm becomes, "Tyranny is every severe deprivation of a natural right, as determined to be a natural right by the people."

Later, in lending his support to the Bill of Rights, Madison inserted a requirement that there should be "no serious objections" to which rights will be included. If there are no serious objections to the voiced identification of a right, then consent can be assumed. The designating of natural rights would be limited by considerable objections that were raised. The fact that Madison wanted there to be no serious objections to the rights included in the Bill of Rights may be indicative of his lukewarm reception of them. Perhaps he thought this would prevent them from being attached to the Constitution, but it is more plausible that he simply wanted every right included to be one about which there were no serious controversies. Nevertheless, in order for natural rights to be listed in the Bill of Rights they would have to undergo a strenuous test (Madison 1977, 12:199; Morgan 1988, 131-59).

An obvious problem that results from the contention that there should be "no serious objections" is that there will obviously be some serious objections. If these objections are intense and sustained, the particular right in question will have to be rejected. That is why Madison, along with the other Founders, constructed a system of proposal and ratification that required strong majority concurrence at both levels. They expected disagreement to occur over what these rights would be, and they took steps to ensure that all of these rights would have the opportunity to be fully revealed to members of Congress and the states, so that all objections could be answered. The layered process necessary to add rights to the Bill of Rights through amendment is demonstrative of the type of system that would preclude new rights from being easily attached.

Regarding Madison's comment that there should be "no serious objection" to the rights listed in the Bill of Rights, I think that a "serious" objection would be an objection that is more than a mere passing fancy or rhetorical doubt. It would have to be a firm and steady disagreement with the content and meaning of the proposed right which is about to be affirmed. This type of objection would need to flow from concerns that the submitted right would act to threaten or destroy other rights or essential interests. If these criteria are met, a serious objection will clearly have been leveled. Given the addition by Madison that there should be "no serious objection" (1977, 12:199) to rights that are given constitutional protection, I believe the reconstructed definition of tyranny by Madison, Dahl, and Beahm should state that "tyranny is every severe deprivation of a natural right, as determined to be a natural right by the people, with no serious objections."

James S. Fishkin, in *Tyranny and Legitimacy*, also determines that Madison and his contemporaries drew their comprehension of natural rights from elements of the Declaration of Independence. It proposed that there were "inherent" or "inalienable rights" requiring protection from any legitimate government, and if those rights were denied by the government it was an "intolerable oppression or tyranny." These rights defined "the very purpose of government," and its "fundamental aim" should be the "preservation of those rights" (1979, 12).

Despite the Declaration's recognition of natural rights, it does not help to define fully what Madison understood them to be. Fishkin, in agreement with Dahl's reconstruction of Madison's definition of tyranny, concludes that Madison was inadequate in his definition of tyranny, in large part because he failed to define natural rights. Fishkin also agrees with Dahl that even if Madison's definition of natural rights could be clarified, the considerable problem of knowing what a "severe deprivation" of those rights would be is unclear, at best. Both he and Dahl come to the view that "at a minimum, any curtailment of natural rights without one's 'consent' was a sufficiently severe deprivation to constitute tyranny" (Dahl 1956, 7).

The conclusion Fishkin comes to is that no matter what the government would do to protect each individual's natural rights, they may still "conflict irreconcilably in particular cases." Fishkin accepts Dahl's view that Madison's definition implies that "any curtailment of natural rights without 'consent' " was a severe deprivation of those rights. Therefore, it is Fishkin's belief that under Dahl's reconstructed definition of Madison, any policy choices the government would make would result in some severe deprivations of natural rights, and thereby, tyranny. His response to this predicament is to accept that some deprivation of natural rights is likely to occur when interests clash, but there need not be a severe deprivation of those rights when they do, at least in most cases. What Fishkin attempts to do is weigh the intensity of competing interests (much like Dahl had done in *A Preface to Democratic Theory*, chap. 4) in order to determine whose natural rights would be most severely deprived if they lost out in a confrontation with other interests. Those who would lose the most should be the most protected from severe deprivation of their natural rights. In some cases it would be easy to determine which interest had the most to lose; in others it would be almost impossible (Fishkin 1979, 13-17).

When the government can avoid "imposing severe deprivations," it, of course, should (Fishkin 1979, 18). Fishkin elaborates on this position by stating, "1. A policy choice by the government is an instance of simple tyranny when that policy imposes severe deprivations even though an alternative policy would have imposed no severe deprivations on anyone" (Fishkin 1979, 18). He uses the phrase "simple tyranny" to separate cases that are clear and uncontested from those that are not. These are cases where tyranny could be "entirely" avoided without a severe deprivation of someone's natural rights (1979, 18-19).

Fishkin adds further clarification to his concept of tyranny by refining his definition of severe deprivation as follows: "2. A severe deprivation is the destruction of an essential interest" (19). By this definition of severe deprivation essential interests would be protected, but there would be cases where the interests would not be essential, and cases where the deprivation would not be severe. Moreover, there will also be cases where every "alternative policy imposes severe deprivations on someone." Fishkin's definition of severe deprivation does not, in the end, eliminate all severe deprivations of natural rights, it only hopes to limit the most "horrendous ones" (1979, 19).

Two problems are still unsolved from Fishkin's definition of severe deprivation. He does not define what he means by destruction, or by essential interests. If a severe deprivation is considered to be the destruction of an "essential interest," as Fishkin states (Fishkin 1979, 19), then perhaps all three definitional problems can be dealt with at one time by elaborating on what essential interests are.

How "essential interest" is defined is key to a clearly structured definition of tyranny. Fishkin, as previously indicated, builds his argument on the intensity of interests. He divides these interests into two categories: "private-regarding interests" and "public-regarding interests." Private-regarding interests have to do with what someone wants for himself, and public-regarding interests have to do with what someone wants for others, or the "state of affairs" (1979, 26-27).

Fishkin believes that both of these interests can be boiled down into private-regarding interests, because they are about what we want, either for others or for ourselves. Private-regarding interests are essential interests. From this he determines that what we want makes up our "life plan." A life plan is, substantially, "the constellation of private-regarding wants and courses of action" to which one is committed. A decisive defeat of this life plan is the destruction of an essential interest. While a decisive defeat of a personal life plan is defined as the destruction of an essential interest, the decisive defeat of a number of individual life plans that were identical, or very similar, would also be a destruction of essential interests (Fishkin 1979, 26-32). Fishkin thinks that a decisive defeat of a life plan can come about in two ways: by one's personal life plan being decisively defeated, or by important parts of one's personal life plan being reversed to the point that it cannot be "fully compensated by the fulfillment of any of his other private-regarding wants" (29-30). Even if we consider that interests are shared by individuals, the decisive defeat of a life plan can be reduced to a private-regarding interest. It is still the individual who suffers. These private-regarding interests invoke the idea of one's right to pursue a life plan. The right to pursue a life plan seems to be derived from one's natural right to do so. Therefore, if a life plan is an essential interest, then an essential interest is a natural right.

If a severe deprivation is the destruction of an essential interest, and an essential interest is in essence a natural right, then it follows that the destruction of an essential interest is the destruction of a natural right. Therefore, the reconstructed definition of tyranny according to Madison, Dahl, Beahm, and Fishkin would state, "Tyranny is every destruction of a natural right, as determined to be a natural right by the people, with no serious objections."

Severe deprivation has been redefined as the destruction of an essential interest, and destruction of an essential interest is the decisive defeat of a life plan. Also, natural rights have been determined to mean essential interest, and an essential interest is understood to be a private-regarding interest.

Other challenges or problems with this definition of tyranny may arise, but it addresses many of the problems in Madison's initial definition of tyranny, while at the same time comporting with the intent of his original definition. Madison did not specifically define tyranny of the majority, but his definition of tyranny has been constructed in such a fashion so as to imply the concept. This latest revision of his definition is directly applicable to the idea of the tyranny of the majority, but it also addresses tyranny that could be perpetrated by a minority against a majority faction. There will be further examination of the definition of tyranny as it applies to the concept of the tyranny of the majority from the other theorists inspected in this study, but this is how Madison's reconstructed definition of tyranny stands for now. To further understand how Madison thought about the tyranny of the majority, a complete evaluation of his view of rights requires attention.

Madison's Perception of Rights

In an attempt to answer the question of why the confederation of states could be "superseded without the unanimous consent of the parties to it," Madison states:

> The first question is answered at once by recurring to the absolute necessity of the case; to the great principle of self-preservation; to the transcendent law of nature and of nature's God, which declares that the safety and happiness of society are the objects at which all political institutions aim and to which all such institutions must be sacrificed (Madison 1961, *Federalist 43*:279).

His answer, in part, is based in natural law, which he believes provides the underlying principles necessary to construct political institutions which will serve the purposes and needs of a civil society, of which "safety and happiness" are paramount. As with many of the Founding Fathers (Rossiter 1953, 363-401), Madison's political theory evolves from the use of the idea of a state of nature as a point of reference and departure (Madison 1961, *Federalist 51*:324), into a subtle acceptance of the notion of natural law. The state of nature was a place wherein anarchy reigned due to the absence of law. Natural law provided guiding moral principles that were consistent in the state of nature, and later formed a basis from which humans could build positive law (Rossiter 1953, 366).

Natural law, according to Rossiter, came to apply or mean four different things to colonial political theorists. First, natural law supplied "a set of moral standards governing private conduct." Rules governing human behavior were thought to be discerned by way of "reason, experience, or revelation" (Rossiter, 1953, 368). During colonial times these rules were basically reduced to the Golden Rule: "Therefore all things whatsoever ye would that men should do to you, do ye even so to them: for this is the law and the prophets" (Matthew 7:12). If people were to follow this prescription, "prosperity and happiness" would be theirs. If they did not follow the Golden Rule, "adversity and sadness" were sure to follow. "The virtuous life was the natural life, just as good government was natural government" (Rossiter 1953, 368).

Second, natural law was a "system of abstract justice" that the laws of men should heed. Positive law that does not conform with natural law is "not only bad law but no law at all." Proposed legislation that offended this sense of abstract justice could not be allowed to stand. A system of government was credible if, and only if, it attended to the enduring laws of nature (Rossiter 1953, 368-69).

Third, in America natural law also became "a line of demarcation around the proper sphere of political authority." If government pressed beyond the scope of this authority it risked "resistance of even revolution." Constitutions needed to be "an earthly replica of natural law," and if they were not they were considered to be "both unconstitutional and unnatural." Guardians of the law were required to "apply whatever sanctions they had at their command" to enforce the constructs that natural law provided (Rossiter 1953, 369).

Fourth, "natural law was the source of natural rights." It was essential that citizens have a steadfast defense of their fundamental rights that emanated from somewhere other than the government itself, in order that they be protected from governmental abrogation of those rights. Natural law, being derived from God or nature, endowed citizens with this defense. Of course, this meant that authorities had to accept readily that this "higher law did exist, and in America, they did. The idea had been a part of common thought since the "first settlements." As put by Rossiter: "In the final reckoning, natural law came to be equated with natural rights" (Rossiter 1953, 369).

The political theory of the American revolutionary period was characterized by the predominance of natural rights doctrine. Natural rights served the practical purpose of providing every man, regardless of his place in society, with the same rights he had brought with him from the state of nature, and these rights could not be surrendered. These rights had become an integral part of society and government and were understood as the rights that belonged "to man as man." The political theory of the time made the distinction between natural law and natural rights obscure at best, because "natural law was all but swallowed up in natural rights" (Rossiter 1953, 375-76).

Despite the fact that Madison does not dwell on the subject of natural law or natural rights, they are both at the root of his political theory (Matthews 1995, 59-63). The problem is that humans far too often are inadequate in comprehending, and therefore expressing, nature's law. Madison grasps the problems inherent in attempting to communicate human ideas in line ‚with natural law and natural rights, and discusses this dilemma in the context of understanding the human mind and the natural world in general. Madison relates that even the "faculties of the mind itself have never yet been distinguished and defined," and that "the great kingdom of nature" has never been clearly revealed to man in spite of his intensive inquiries. Madison attributes some of the difficulties faced at the Constitutional Convention to this inability to clearly communicate the natural laws of the universe (Madison 1961, 37:227-28).

The difficulty faced when attempting to distinguish the natural division of power between the national government and the state governments provides an example of just how arduous a task detecting natural law and natural rights can be. In the natural world distinctions are difficult enough, but when it comes to making distinctions in the political world, problems are exacerbated. Madison states that:

> When we pass from the works of nature, in which all the delineations are perfectly accurate and appear to be otherwise only from the imperfection of the eye which surveys them, to the institutions of man, in which the obscurity arises as well from the object itself as from the organ by which it is contemplated, we must perceive the necessity of moderating still further our expectations and hopes from the efforts of human sagacity. Experience has instructed us that no skill in the science of government has yet been able to discriminate and define, with sufficient certainty, its three great provinces—the legislative, executive, and judiciary; or even the privileges and powers of the different legislative branches. Questions daily occur in the course of practice which prove the obscurity which reigns in these subjects, and which puzzle the greatest adepts in political science (Madison 1961, 37:228).

It is a wonder to Madison that the convention produced the outcome that it did. He, somewhat surprisingly, states:

> The real wonder is that so many difficulties should have been surmounted, and surmounted with a unanimity almost as unprecedented as it must have been unexpected. . . . It is impossible for the man of pious reflection not to perceive in it a finger of that Almighty hand which has been so frequently and signally extended to our relief in the critical stages of the revolution (Madison 1961, 37:230-31).

What is surprising here is that Madison would make so much of the unanimity of the convention when there was so much dissention, especially early on. What is not a surprise is that he attributes their success to the "Almighty." This is in keeping with his theoretical contention that there is a more fundamental law at work. Madison obviously thought that the results of the convention were caused by some force that could direct human beings to create a government that reflected natural law, or God's law.

Madison does not indicate directly that he thought natural rights could not be defined, but by his own words he certainly had doubts about the ability of humans to ascertain clearly what natural rights could be derived from natural law. Even though Madison shared many of the same general ideas about natural rights with the revolutionary-period political theorists, he also knew that there was great disagreement among them, as evidenced by the difficulty involved in arriving at the Bill of Rights. He apprehended how important rights were to

some of the Founders (not the least of whom was Jefferson), and many in the
public at large, by the intensity with which the Bill of Rights was argued.
Madison's motivation to support the Bill of Rights stems, in part, from his effort
to squelch an attempt by Anti-Federalists to defeat ratification of the
Constitution by complaints that fundamental rights were not adequately
protected within the body of the Constitution (Morgan, 134-38). Madison's
somewhat begrudging support can be found in a letter to Jefferson on the
subject. He states:

> My own opinion has always been in favor of a bill of rights; provided it be so
> framed as not to imply powers not meant to be included in the enumeration. At
> the same time I have never thought the omission a material defect, nor been
> anxious to supply it even by subsequent amendment, for any other reason than
> that it is anxiously desired by others. I have favored it because I supposed it
> might be of use, and if properly executed could not be of disservice (Madison
> 1977, 11:297).

Madison goes on to list four reasons why he had "not viewed" the Bill of
Rights "in an important light." The fourth reason is relevant to the case being
made here (1977, 297-98). He argues that "experience proves the inefficacy of a
bill of rights on those occasions when its control is most needed. Repeated
violations of these parchment barriers have been committed by overbearing
majorities in every State. In Virginia I have seen the bill of rights violated in
every instance where it has been opposed to a popular current" (297-98).

The salient point to be derived from Madison regarding the previous
statements is that identifying rights does not necessarily serve to protect them.
The historical record, as Madison relates it, indicates that specifying rights has
done no good in preserving them.

In contradiction to these statements, Madison later turns his four arguments
against specifying rights through the Bill of Rights into a willingness to support
their enumeration. He realizes that while paper barriers may be too weak to
prevent tyrannical majorities from violating rights, they do have a "tendency to
impress some degree of respect for them, to establish public opinion in their
favor, and to rouse the attention of the whole community" (Madison 1977,
12:204-5).

Madison had seemingly changed his mind about whether declaring rights
openly could deter oppressive majorities, but he had acquiesced to declaring
rights in order to make the Constitution more attractive to the states that hadn't
ratified it. He also thought that it was necessary to proceed with caution, because
he would be "unwilling to see a door opened for a re-consideration of the whole
structure of the government" (Madison 1977, 12:196-99; Morgan 1988, 138).

From these conflicting opinions I believe it is at least fair to say that
Madison wavered in his support for expressly itemizing rights. He did not
abstain or dissent, in the end, from asserting these rights, as long as there was
"no serious objection" to them, support had been expressed overtly for them,

and "Congress and three-fourths of the states" were in all probability going to approve them (Madison 1977, 12:196-99; Morgan 1988, 138). From these criteria it is evident that Madison thought it best for the people, or their designated representatives and delegates, to decide which rights should be enunciated. Although he played an important part in the determination of which rights would be put forth, he was reluctant to say which ones should be identified, for fear of leaving out some of the most important ones. In short, natural rights were what the public said they were (Morgan, 1988, 131-59). It would be helpful to his definition of tyranny if Madison had defined natural rights sufficiently that the parameters of his meaning could be positively discerned, but as Dahl notes, Madison was:

> up to his ears in politics, advising, persuading, softening the harsh word, playing down this difficulty and exaggerating that, engaging in debate, harsh controversy, polemics, and sly maneuver (1956, 5).

However, I find there is reason to believe that he didn't think it was his job to circumscribe which natural rights should be elevated to "inalienable" status. Natural rights doctrine contends that natural rights are what the governed determine them to be, as they are able to conceive them (Declaration of Independence). Although this is always a precarious business, it is nonetheless their choice to make. Madison remained vague in defining natural rights, not only because he was astute as a politician, but because he was perspicacious enough as a political theorist to know that rights will be decided upon by each society, as it is competent to detect them.

To ensure that rights are protected, Madison found it necessary to provide barriers to majoritarian tyranny. His conceptualization of how to correct for tyrannical majorities relies on governmental power when social checks (like factions balancing each other out) are not sufficient to the task. The devices that Madison relies on are multiple and varied.

Madison's Corrections to the Tyranny of the Majority

The need to control the effects of majority factions is left to the government, according to Madison. It is clear that when a majority faction cannot be balanced by the republican principle of majority rule, the government itself must have safeguards in place to cool the heated passions of a mob mentality. Madison accurately recognizes that "if a majority be united by a common interest, the rights of the minority will be insecure" (Madison 1961, 51:323).

Government is not the hoped-for solution, because the preferred answer to the problem is that factions will tend to cancel each other out (Madison 1961, 51:323-25). When republican remedies of popular sovereignty do not suffice then republican governmental devices are engaged to provide a cure.

Madison is all too aware that majoritarian principles can produce anarchy as well as injustice. He supports the axiom that the people rule, but he tempers it with alternative corrections, if they are needed. Madison states that "in framing a government which is to be administered by men over men, the great difficulty lies in this: you must first enable the government to control the governed; and in the next place oblige it to control itself. A dependence on the people is no doubt, the primary control on the government; but experience has taught mankind the necessity of auxiliary precautions" (Madison 1961, 51:322).

Government control of a majority faction is not what is expected but protection against the tyranny of the majority requires it. A government having these powers can develop tyrannical majorities from within. Steps must be taken to ensure that one branch does not begin to tyrannize the others, but also that the government as a whole does not become tyrannical.

The Constitution of the United States, as set forth by Madison and other Founders, has a number of impediments lodged within it to prevent tyrannical majorities from establishing their positions at the expense of minorities. The first of these impediments is the separation of powers. The legislative, executive, and the judicial branches are all given distinct powers. Even the legislature is divided into two houses to prevent an unnecessary centralization of power. Madison states that "the great security against a gradual concentration of the several powers in the same department consists in giving to those who administer each department the necessary constitutional means and personal motives to resist encroachments of the others" (Madison 1961, 51:321-22).

In the *Federalist Papers*, 47 through 51, Madison defends the separation of powers as the bulwark of liberty. It is also the failure to separate the powers of government that is at the very heart of Madison's initial definition of tyranny (1961, 47:301). In addition to the separation of the branches of the government, the government is itself divided between the federal and the state levels. This separation acts to reduce the possibility that government will coalesce and use its authority to tyrannize the citizens. Separation will also cause each division to be wary of the other. Madison asserts:

> In the compound republic of America, the power surrendered by the people is first divided between two distinct governments, and then the portion allotted to each subdivided among distinct and separate departments. Hence a double security arises to the rights of the people. The different governments will control each other, at the same time that each will be controlled by itself (1961, 51:323).

Further commenting on the effect a federal republic will have on protecting both individuals and minorities, Madison states:

> "Whilst all authority in it will be derived from and dependent on the society, the society itself will be broken into so many parts, interests and classes of citizens, that the rights of individuals, or of the minority, will be in little danger from interested combinations of the majority" (*Federalist 51*:324).

Some have raised questions about whether Madison supported a view of federalism that backed nationalist tendencies or secretly longed for states to have considerable autonomy in the new republic (Greene 1994). Although Madison did regret the fact that the convention did not allow the national government veto rights over state legislation (Madison 1977, 10:212), he can most accurately be characterized as only a moderate nationalist (Greene 1994, 60). He was convinced that a "constitutional negative on the laws of the States" seemed necessary to protect individuals from "encroachments on their rights." Nonetheless, it was not "complete subordination" that he sought but only "a safeguard against state malfeasance" (Green 1994, 61).

Beyond the separation of powers acting as an impediment to tyrannical majorities, checks and balances were set in place at the convention to allow each branch not only its own power but the power to place a negative on the other branches. The concept of checks and balances connects the branches by making them dependent on one another. When one acts the others have the power to counteract it. This keeps all branches cognizant of the attitudes and predisposition of the other branches. In order to bring about a particular governmental policy, cooperation and compromise are essential. Minority protections are elevated by the necessity of this interplay between competing interests.

Congress can check the executive and the judicial branches in a number of different ways, but it has two forms of internal checks that are different from the others. First, the Senate can filibuster, which impedes action by the legislature when a significant minority acts to deter or delay passage of legislation (the required number of members of the Senate needed to filibuster today is forty-one because a three-fifths majority is needed to bring about cloture, which is the ending of a filibuster). Second, by a function of the separation of powers, the legislature is bicameral, but this also acts as a check on itself, because one house cannot pass legislation without concurrence from the other. This was done in the legislature because the threat of the tyranny of the majority within the government was thought to be the greatest in that body (Madison 1961, 51:322-23). The justification for this belief is that representatives, being popularly elected (the Senate's members were chosen by their state legislatures until 1913 and the Seventeenth Amendment), are more directly connected to the whim of the people. If a majority of the people choose to exercise their will through their vote and place in office a number of representatives in Congress who reflect that will, there is nothing to stop them.

An electoral check on Congress is that the two houses are elected on different schedules. The members of the House of Representatives are elected every two years (this makes them the more susceptible to the influence of tyrannical majorities), and the members of the Senate are elected every six. However, senatorial elections are staggered, and only one-third of the Senate seats are up for election every two years. The staggered elections in the Senate were employed to cool the passions of oppressive majorities.

The external checks that were assigned to Congress are: it can elect the president and the vice president if the Electoral College fails to produce a winner; the Senate confirms presidential elections by the Electoral College; Congress can override a presidential veto with a two-thirds majority in both houses; the Senate has the power of confirmation over presidential appointments to his cabinet and the courts; the Senate also offers advice and consent on treaties; Congress can propose amendments to the Constitution by a two-thirds majority in both houses; the House can impeach judges and presidents; the Senate holds trials on removal after impeachments, where a two-thirds majority is necessary to remove; only Congress can declare war; through the War Powers Act of 1973 Congress can demand that presidents show cause after sixty days why troops should remain in a hostile environment.

The executive branch is electorally checked in a couple of ways. The Electoral College, whose vote is determined by popular vote within the states, elects the president. As mentioned above, if this fails Congress selects the president. The president serves four-year terms and is limited to two terms, or less than ten years by the Twenty-second Amendment.

The checks that the president can exercise are: he can veto legislation; he can set the time for adjournment of Congress if it fails to agree on a time; judges are appointed to the courts by the president; as commander in chief of the military the president can wage war.

There is no electoral check on the judiciary since they are appointed by the president and confirmed by the Senate. The power of judicial review is probably the greatest power the courts have, wherein they can declare acts of government officials unconstitutional. This power was firmly entrenched by the case of *Marbury v. Madison*, in 1803.

This list of checks and balances may not be exhaustive, but it does point out the many protections within the government against the tyranny of the majority, as well as protections against minority tyranny. Madison is unique in that he had the opportunity to participate in the creation of these protections. He was able to discuss and debate the pros and cons of inserting these ideas in the Constitution. He continued to work and write as he served in various offices throughout the government, which gave him insights as to how well the instrument that he had helped to construct functioned. The question is, are these protections adequate to deter tyranny of the majority?

Most of the protections against tyranny of the majority have been helpful in preventing it. However, the one protection that Madison wanted but did not get deserves further attention. The notion of a national veto over state legislation is the one item requiring additional investigation. Madison's "chief regret" was that the Convention did not provide "the new government an all-purpose power to veto state legislation" (Greene 1994, 57). He thought the "mutability of the laws of the States" a "serious evil." He further contended that these "evils" had contributed to the "uneasiness which produced the Convention" (Madison 1977, 10:212).

That Madison felt strongly about a veto over state laws is a good indication that it may have served a positive purpose. The evidence of state laws tyrannizing minorities is substantial: literacy tests administered to blacks in the South, citizenship tests being required of communists, and state-sanctioned Christian prayers being read in public schools are all examples. Of course Madison didn't know of these "evils," but he understood that local prejudices could greatly increase the chances that minorities would suffer a plethora of tyrannies. Therefore, I believe that Madison was right; the addition of a national veto over state legislation would be a defensible guard against majoritarian oppression.

One practical concern that does present itself regarding a national veto over state laws is how Congress would find the time to review all state laws to determine their acceptability. This would incur a considerable expense and devotion of time and talent. Although the investment may well be worth it, the present application of the supremacy clause (Article VI, U.S. Constitution) may be a reasonably efficient way of overriding state laws that directly clash with national laws, the Constitution, or violations of the U.S. Bill of Rights (*McCulloch v. Maryland* 1819).

That having been said, it is still difficult to ignore the desires of Madison. His concern throughout the convention was to build into the Constitution protections for minorities that would otherwise have been trampled under the feet of majoritarians. The fact that he was able to insert into the Constitution many of the aforementioned protections is a testimony to his keen insight and understanding of human fallibility as it might reveal itself in a democratic republic. No doubt he and the other Founders were protecting their own financial interests (Beard 1913), but in the process of doing so they did not make it impossible for others to succeed in their endeavors. To the contrary, they made it more likely that citizens would have opportunities not yet available anywhere else in the world (Wood 1991).

References

Beard, Charles A. 1913. *An Economic Interpretation of the Constitution of the United States.* New York: The Free Press.

Bill of Rights. First Ten Amendments to the U.S. Constitution.

Dahl, Robert A. 1956. *A Preface to Democratic Theory.* Chicago: The University of Chicago Press.

Declaration of Independence.

Fishkin, James S. 1979. *Tyranny and Legitimacy: A Critique of Political Theories.* Baltimore: Johns Hopkins University Press.

Greene, Francis R. 1994. "Madison's View of Federalism." *Publius: The Journal of Federalism.* Winter 1994. Vol. 24, No. 1: 47-61.

Madison, James. 1953. *The Complete Madison: His Basic Writings.* Ed. and with an introduction by Saul K. Padover. New York: Harper & Brothers.

Madison, James. With Alexander Hamilton, and John Jay. 1961. *The Federalist Papers*. Introduction by Clinton Rossiter. New York: New American Library.

————. 1966. *Notes of Debates in the Federal Convention of 1787*. With an introduction by Adrienne Koch. Athens: Ohio University Press.

————. 1977. *The Papers of James Madison*. Ed. Robert A. Rutland, Charles F. Hobson, William M. E. Rachal, and Jeanne K. Sisson. Fifteen volumes to date. Charlottesville: University Press of Virginia.

Marbury v. Madison. 1 Cranch. 137 (1803).

Matthews, Richard K. 1995. *If Men Were Angels: James Madison and the Heartless Empire of Reason*. Lawrence: University Press of Kansas.

McCulloch v. Maryland. 4 Wheat. 316 (1819).

Morgan, Robert J. 1988. *James Madison on the Constitution and the Bill of Rights*. Contributions in Legal Studies, No. 48. New York: Greenwood Press.

Nelson, Brian R. 1996. *Western Political Thought: From Socrates to the Age of Ideology*. 2nd ed. Englewood Cliffs, NJ: Prentice Hall. Inc.

Rossiter, Clinton. 1953. *Seedtime of the Republic: The Origin of the American Tradition of Political Liberty*. New York: Harcourt, Brace.

————. 1963. *The Political Thought of the American Revolution*. New York: Harcourt, Brace.

United States Constitution.

Wood, Gordon S. 1991. *The Radicalism of the American Revolution*. New York: Vintage Books.

Chapter 3

Tocqueville

Tocqueville addresses the issue of the tyranny of the majority from a different perspective. As a Frenchman he is perhaps able to see the United States from a more objective point of view. He looks to the populace for the causes of tyranny of the majority and finds that social conditions have a great deal to do with the problem. He also finds possible solutions to majority tyranny that others did not see, and still might take issue with. Therefore, I believe Tocqueville is an important contributor to the subject and deserves serious attention.

Tocqueville's Tyranny of the Majority

The source of legitimate authority in democratic governments, according to Tocqueville, is the will of the majority. "The absolute sovereignty of the will of the majority is the essence of democratic government, for in democracies there is nothing outside the majority capable of resisting it" (1969, 1: 246).

The moral authority vested in the majority is based on the ideas that "there is more enlightenment and wisdom in a numerous assembly than in a single man," and "that the interest of the greatest number should be preferred to that of those who are fewer." The power of the majority takes time to establish itself as being legitimate, but in the United States it came not only to be well respected but also it has "passed into mores and affects even the smallest habits of life" (1969, 1: 247).

The majority is respected because everyone hopes to be a part of it at some time. This sanctioning of the majority lends even more authority to its power:

Hence the majority in the United States has immense actual power and a power of opinion which is almost as great. When once its mind is made up on any question, there are, so to say, no obstacles which can retard, much less halt, its

27

progress and give it time to hear the wails of those it crushes as it passes. The consequences of this state of affairs are fate-laden and dangerous for the future (Tocqueville 1969, 1: 248).

If the majority is respected too much, the danger exists for all, because most everyone will be a part of the minority at some point. If the minority point of view is diminished too far, the motivation for protecting it will be minimal, if it exists at all. Not allowing for points of view that are contrary to popularly held beliefs eventually leads to limits in free thinking. Once limits in thinking have developed then limits to the solution of problems have been imposed ipso facto (Boesche 1996, 219-21).

Regarding government, the ill of excessive majoritarianism is most prevalent in the legislatures of democratic governments. Tocqueville states, "Two main dangers threaten the existence of democracies: Complete subjection of the legislative power to the will of the electoral body. Concentration of all the other powers of government in the hands of the legislative power" (1969, 155).

Legislatures are inherently unstable because "it is the nature of democracies to bring new men to power." If legislators are given great power, the likelihood of the public's every whim being carried into the lawmaking function is increased. "In America the lawmaking authority has been given sovereign power." Laws can be passed quickly, and the legislators who pass these laws are changed frequently, producing the most volatile and unstable of democratic conditions (Tocqueville 1969, 248-50; Schleifer 1980, 220). As Tocqueville sees it, "The omnipotence of the majority and the rapid as well as absolute manner in which its decisions are executed in the United States not only make the law unstable but have a like effect on the execution of the law and on public administrative activity" (1969, 1:249).

Projects are taken up with great enthusiasm in order to please the majority. Once these projects have been substantially addressed, their continuance is largely ignored because new projects have captured the attention of the public. Oversight of ongoing concerns is largely ignored by the legislature because the focus has been turned to the new fancy of the majority. Therefore, the administrative aspects of governmental functioning are seldom reviewed by the legislature, making for less than adequate administration of continuing projects, programs, and the facilities that carry them out (Tocqueville 1969, 249-50).

This yearning to satisfy the will of the majority which characterizes democracy puts Tocqueville in the contradictory position of both despising the notion that the majority is all powerful and yet understanding that it is the source of all power in democratic societies. "I regard it as an impious and detestable maxim that in matters of government the majority of a people has the right to do everything, and nevertheless I place the origin of all powers in the will of the majority. Am I in contradiction with myself?" (1969, 1: 250).

He resolves this contradiction by turning to a more fundamental law which is upheld by "the majority of all men," not just the majority of certain societies.

"That law is justice," and it is justice which "forms the boundary to each people's right" (1969, 1: 250).

Tocqueville equates a nation to a jury which is "entrusted to represent universal society and to apply the justice which is its law." He does not believe the jury (nation) should have more power than the society (world) to determine how the laws will be applied. In other words, no society should perceive itself as having the authority to elevate any decision above what is just. If the will of the majority in a certain society is elevated to a level of greater reverence than that of justice, then all citizens are in danger of losing their freedom by way of the majoritarian tyrants (1969, 1: 250-51):

> There are those not afraid to say that in matters which only concern itself a nation cannot go completely beyond the bounds of justice and reason and that there is therefore no need to fear giving total power to the majority representing it. But that is the language of a slave. What is the majority, in its collective capacity, if not an individual with opinions, and usually with interests, contrary to those of another individual, called the minority? Now, if you admit that a man vested with omnipotence can abuse it against his adversaries, why not admit the same concerning a majority? Have men, by joining together, changed their character? By becoming stronger, have they become more patient of obstacles? For my part, I cannot believe that, and I will never grant to several that power to do everything which I refuse to a single man (Tocqueville 1969, 1: 252).

As with Madison, Tocqueville perceives the threat of tyranny as coming originally from the people. But eventually the government may become tyrannical as the citizens are lulled into complacency by the fact that they have done their democratic duty and elected officials who support their opinions. Therein lies the rub. Opinions of individuals have too often been shaped by the desire to jump on the bandwagon once the majority opinion is clear. Since citizens perceive themselves to be equal, holding a different opinion than the majority is a threat to this recognized and respected authority. "In America the majority has enclosed thought within a formidable fence." (Tocqueville 1969, 2:690-95, 1:254-56, 1:57, 2:435-36; Schleifer 1980, 191-223).

In an attempt to characterize Tocqueville's concerns about the effects of majority opinion on the minority, German researcher Elisabeth Noelie-Neumann has suggested that a "spiral of silence" results from the fear people experience when they perceive that their opinions do not conform with those of the majority. As individuals who hold minority opinions silence themselves, they also isolate themselves from the public. This isolation further silences dissenting opinions and drives a wider wedge between the majority and the minority. Actions that may result from this spiral of silence can lead to a breakdown in the protections against majority tyranny (Noelle-Neumann 1984).

Barbara Allen's interpretation of Tocqueville on the subject of how majority opinion affects minorities focuses more on the political designs of authority that cause a spiral of silence, which result in political and social isolation. She believes that "Tocqueville was concerned that American federalism provided too few safeguards against the tendency of centralization." She states:

> Tocqueville would direct our attention to an empirical investigation of the centralization of intellectual authority and the change in forums for public expression of ideas. By understanding more about the structure of authority in which communication occurs, particularly in cross-cultural investigations of these phenomenon, we can better understand the importance of events that result in a spiral of silence (Allen 1991, 267).

Majority opinion plays a key role in the centralization of power. If diverse forums for gathering and dispersing information do not exist, then majority opinion will continue to minimize minority positions. The spiral of silence will continue to occur as citizens feel evermore compelled to accept majority opinion as a part of their need to be equal.

Equality, while an important virtue in a democratic republic, can be taken to an extreme where freedom to hold different opinions is not tolerated and sameness is required. Tocqueville feared that equality may be elevated to this extreme, making public opinion sacrosanct. If public officials are elected with the expectation that they will reflect popular opinion, then not only will the officials be carrying out policy that may reflect the public's desire for sameness, but eventually the people will pay less attention to their officials, leaving them greater opportunity to tyrannize over their constituents (Tocqueville 1969, 1:57, 254-56, 2:690-95; Nelson 1996, 298-304; Commager 1993, 24-25; Boesche 1987, 150-52). Tocqueville states, "I know no country in which, speaking generally, there is less independence of mind and true freedom of discussion than in America" (1969, 1:254-55).

He further complains, "The majority in the United States takes over the business of supplying the individual with a quantity of ready-made opinions and so relieves him of the necessity of forming his own. So there are many theories of philosophy, morality, and politics which everyone adopts unexamined on the faith of public opinion (1969, 2:435-36).

The sameness that predominates in public opinion as a result of the people desiring equality also comes about by the need of all people to accept a number of things in their life that they don't have time to examine. Tocqueville realizes that agreement is necessary to any common belief, and that if a people are to govern themselves, concurrence on a number of issues is helpful in this endeavor. In order for societies to manage their public affairs, common ideas and common action need to exist, or "there could be nobody social" (Tocqueville 1969, 2:434-35). Even if a man lived alone, needing to prove truth in every matter would be endless.

The problem with common ideas becoming too readily accepted is that they "become a sort of religion with the majority as its prophet" (Tocqueville 1969, 2:436).

Intellectual authority will not come from the despot, but from the majority insisting on acceptance of their ideas. This limitation may well lead to a loss of dignity for the individual and a reduction in the "happiness of mankind"(2:436). The new despot may become the "general will of the greatest number" (2:436), if equality induces men to "freely give up thinking at all" (2:436). Tocqueville asserts:

> If democratic peoples substituted the absolute power of a majority for all the various powers that used excessively to impede or hold back the upsurge of individual thought, the evil itself would only have changed its form. Men would by no means have found the way to live in independence; they would only have succeeded in the difficult task of giving slavery a new face. . . . I am little concerned to know who it is that oppressed me; I am no better inclined to pass my head under the yoke because a million men hold it for me (Tocqueville 1969, 2: 436).

Public opinion is the method by which tyranny is perpetrated against individuals and society at large, while the lusting for equality is the cause of majority tyranny. Tocqueville states:

> The citizen of a democracy comparing himself with the others feels proud of his equality with each. But when he compares himself with all his fellows and measures himself against this vast entity, he is overwhelmed by a sense of his insignificance and weakness. The same equality which makes him independent of each separate citizen leaves him isolated and defenseless in the face of the majority. So in democracies public opinion has a strange power of which aristocratic nations can form no conception. It uses no persuasion to forward its beliefs, but by some mighty pressure of the mind of all upon the intelligence of each it imposes its ideas and makes them penetrate men's very souls (1969, 2: 435).

The overwhelming desire of democratic peoples for equality in the extreme destroys freedom (Nelson 1996, 299). It is not because democratic people do not love freedom, or liberty, that they have a natural inclination for it. What they want is "equality in freedom, and if they cannot have that, they still want equality in slavery" (Tocqueville 1969, 2:506).

Democratic peoples will tolerate many difficulties to safeguard equality because "it is equality for which they feel an eternal love" (Tocqueville 1969, 1: 57). Those who attempt to interfere with the people maintaining equality will be removed from power in one fashion or another. However, when citizens are truly equal, "it becomes difficult to defend their freedom from the encroachments of power"(1:57). The paradox is that freedom cannot exist without equality because it allows individuals to choose their paths in life from the authority it brings them to do so; but tyranny in a democratic society is not likely to occur without equality (2:503-06).

Tocqueville understood that this type of tyranny was something new in the world.

> Thus I think that the type of oppression which threatens democracies is different from anything there has ever been in the world before. Our contemporaries will find no prototype of it in their memories. I have myself vainly searched for a word which will exactly express the whole of the conception I have formed. Such old words as "despotism" and "tyranny" do not fit. The thing is new, and as I cannot find a word for it I must try to define it (1969, 2:691).

He further describes this new oppression by stating that "it would be more widespread and milder; it would degrade men rather than torment them" (1969, 2:691).

What Tocqueville was describing is how the government will begin to absorb ever greater power as its citizens are lulled into believing that their interests are being served by public officials who act more like schoolmasters, dutifully reflecting public opinion. He fears that a democratic society like America is "particularly open to the establishment of despotism" (1969, 2:690). The type of despotism that Tocqueville is referring to is administrative despotism, wherein each citizen participates in his/her own subjection by allowing the government to manage his/her petty affairs. This type of despotism tries to keep the citizens happy by gently ordering their lives in such a way that they have little to complain about, but also little to think about while they are caught up in their daily lives. The government is not overbearing, but Tocqueville contends:

> It provides for their security, foresees and supplies their necessities, facilitates their pleasure, manages their principal concerns, directs their industry, makes rules for their testaments, and divides their inheritances. Why should it not entirely relieve them from the trouble of thinking and all the cares of living? . . . Equality has prepared men for all this, predisposing them to endure it and often even regard it as beneficial (1969, 2:692).

Elections are temporary reprieves from the dullness of the people's lives where they are for a moment masters of the government, but Tocqueville wonders how people who have given up managing their own lives can make a wise choice "of those who are to do that for them" (1969, 2:694). He foresees them trying different systems of elections as if the problem were with the Constitution rather than with themselves; but to no avail. Their lust for equality has left them stripped of true power, and, more importantly of their humanity. Tocqueville proclaims, "I believe that it is easier to establish an absolute and despotic government amongst a people whose social conditions are equal than among any other" (2:695).

The new despot that Tocqueville has envisioned is like no other previously identified. It is "despotism without an identifiable despot." Since there is no despot, there is no need for the usual functionaries of despotism: the advisors, the spies, or the paramilitary forces. This new despotism is constructed by innocent citizens enjoying an equality that has provided them with the freedom to exercise their individuality as never before. Little do they realize that they have laid the foundation for a tyranny that is as dangerous, and as insidious, as any tyranny known to humanity (Boesche 1996, 236).

Tocqueville's Addition to the Definition of Tyranny

The type of tyranny that Tocqueville has described has both quantitative (political) as well as qualitative (social) elements. Tyrannical majorities result from not only quantitative elements that relate to political issues, but from qualitative elements that include social issues. Quantitative elements pertained mostly to votes, both by the people and by their representatives in legislatures. Qualitative elements refer to social issues such as equality, individualism, associations, and public opinion. "The majority not only won votes and determined policies, it also influenced attitudes" (Roper 1989, 17).

Quantitative and qualitative elements intermingle and at times overlap to produce majoritarian tyranny. For example, there are many similarities between public opinion and opinions expressed in the voting booth. Both indicate a preference for certain ideas or candidates, but voting is mostly a political act, while public opinion remains mostly a social phenomenon. Madison introduced the notion that qualitative elements were an integral part of majorities tyrannizing minorities in his discussion of factions (Madison 1961, 10:77-84). However, Tocqueville broadened and made more sophisticated the idea that qualitative elements played a major role in causing majority tyranny.

Qualitative elements, as elaborated on by Tocqueville, add a new dimension to the description of tyranny of the majority, and thereby to the definition of tyranny. The constructed definition of tyranny used in the last chapter combined the ideas of Madison, Dahl, Beahm, and Fishkin. What resulted was the following: "Tyranny is every destruction of a natural right, as determined to be a natural right by the people, with no serious objections."

Tocqueville does not provide a specific definition of tyranny, but in his description of tyranny of the majority he does suggest that a new type of tyranny has broadened the parameters of what tyranny means (1969, 2:691).

If Tocqueville's description of majority tyranny is combined with Roper's characterization of majority tyranny having both quantitative and qualitative elements (1989, 17), a new definition of tyranny can be suggested: "Tyranny is every quantitative and qualitative destruction of a natural right, as determined to be a natural right by the people, with no serious objections."

The inclusion of quantitative and qualitative in the definition of tyranny simply qualifies the type of tyranny that can destroy a natural right. Tyranny can come about in a number of different ways, and the concepts of quantitative and qualitative are inclusive of all conceivable paths to tyranny. As with the previous definition of tyranny, this definition incorporates tyranny of the majority. It is difficult to define "despotism without an identifiable despot" (Boesche 1996, 236) or tyranny without a tyrant. But qualitative elements do help define what despotism/tyranny is in democratic societies. Qualitative elements act to destroy natural rights through different methods than despots/tyrants use, but the results are very similar. Both Tocqueville and Madison put natural rights at the root of what is worth protecting in any civil society. They consider them to have enhanced importance in a democratic society.

Tocqueville's Perception of Rights

According to Lamberti there "is no mention of 'natural rights'" by Tocqueville in his discussion of rights, although natural law "is presented in sketchy fashion without further development" (1989, 75). Zetterbaum, while acknowledging that there is "no thematic presentation of a doctrine of natural rights in Tocqueville," takes note that "he clearly does not altogether free himself from the idea of natural rights" (1967, 39). In fact, during Tocqueville's discussion of political associations he states, "The most natural right of man, after that of acting on his own, is that of combining his efforts with those of his fellows and acting together. Therefore the right of association seems to me by nature almost as inalienable as individual liberty" (1969, 193).

Furthermore, if Rossiter is to be believed, "natural law was the source of natural rights," and in the political theory of the time of the Founders "natural law came to be equated with natural rights" (1953, 360). Tocqueville's view of rights appears to be, at least somewhat, a product of equating the two.

Tocqueville determines that if rights are not adequately appreciated, relations between humans are relegated to struggles of power. Society is elevated by the recognition of rights for citizens, because it is a verification of their ability to behave in an intelligent and responsible manner. America was notable for supporting the idea that all citizens have certain rights. This was considered to be a dangerous proposition during the infancy of a government, or when passions were running high, but Tocqueville thought it was in the best interest of a government to support the needs of society by promoting its rights (Lamberti 1989, 74):

> So, then, when I am told that laws are feeble and the governed turbulent, that passions are lively and virtue powerless, and that in this situation one must not dream of increasing the rights of democracy, I answer that it is for these very reasons that one must consider doing so, and in truth, I think the governments have an even greater interest in doing this than has society, for governments perish but society cannot die (1969, 239).

Tocqueville differentiates between three different ideas of rights: divine, moral, and political. The degeneration of divine and moral rights has left society to rely on political rights which are increasingly tied to private interests. If it is not found to be in the private interest of citizens to advocate political rights, tyranny of some form is the likely outcome:

> Do you not see that religions are growing weak and that the conception of the sanctity of rights is vanishing? Do you not see that mores are changing and that the moral conception of rights is being obliterated with them? Do you not notice how on all sides beliefs are giving way to arguments, and feelings to calculations? If amid this universal collapse you do not succeed in linking the idea of rights to personal interest, which provides the only stable point in the human heart, what other means will be left to you to govern the world, if not fear (Tocqueville 1969, 1:239)?

Of general ideas in the world Tocqueville likes the idea of virtue best. Rights are what he chooses as second best, but the two are mingled. "The idea of rights is nothing but the conception of virtue applied to the world of politics." Rights are what is just and good within a democratic government, as the citizens are given the power to see the just and good. It is by the "idea of rights" that tyranny and license have been defined. Citizens know what the limits are that they can be pushed to, because they have a sense of what their rights are (Tocqueville 1969, 1:237-38). He states:

> No man can be great without virtue, nor any nation great without respect for rights; one might almost say that without it there can be no society, for what is a combination of rational and intelligent beings held together by force alone? (1969, 1:238).

For Tocqueville the "first and most fundamental natural right is individual liberty" (Zetterbaum 1967, 39). Rights both "defined the individual's area of free action" and required a "reciprocal acceptance of limitations on his sphere of action" (Lively 1965, 110). As Lively puts it, "In a democratic society, as the feeling of social obligation weakened, the only way to gain general acceptance of the idea of rights was to connect it with personal interest; and the only way to do this was to give every member of the community the exercise of rights" (1965, 110). The problem with giving all citizens the power to exercise rights is how society then teaches them to use them.

Tocqueville equates the teaching of rights to members of a society to that of teaching children to respect the rights of others. Children have no sense of other people's property because they have not had property themselves and don't appreciate the meaning of it until they have had something of their own. Once they grasp the meaning of owning something they gain an appreciation of the rights of others to their property, because they now know how important their rights to property are. Therefore, adults learn to appreciate rights only after they have ascertained them and comprehended the importance they have in securing their freedom. They do not attack the rights of others because they do not want their rights attacked. The longer a populace has had rights the better it becomes at using them. Tocqueville believes this to be evident in America, where the states that have "enjoyed their rights" the longest are the ones who have become the most adept at their use (1969, 1: 238-40).

American citizens were "invested with political rights" at a time when they were "few and their mores simple." However, as they have grown more powerful they have not "increased the powers of democracy; rather they have extended its domain." Even the least of its citizens has been imbued with the "idea of political rights," promoting both their use and the equality of citizens in a democratic government (Tocqueville 1969, 1:239). The natural rights of all people are derived from their natural equality (Zetterbaum 1987, 781).

Although natural equality provided the springboard for people to claim their natural rights, the exercise of these rights has led to a form of extreme equality in America. The more equal people have become the more they have relied upon their individual capabilities. However, as Tocqueville suggests, "The same equality which makes him independent of each separate citizen leaves him isolated and defenseless in the face of the majority" (1969, 2:435).

The need to form associations becomes imperative in order to protect individual interests, equality, and the rights that are shared by all citizens of the society. Without associations, individuals become increasingly unable to resist "power by themselves," because they have become "isolated and weak." As this separation between individuals grows they lose appreciation for their "common interests" and the necessity of "limiting the power of the state." Associations are a response to the threat in a democratic society of not being able to correct these two problems. "Man's humanity itself is threatened by misguided democratic individualism with its constricted moral view " (Lamberti 1989, 82).

> The morals and intelligence of a democratic people would be in as much danger as its commerce and industry if ever a government wholly usurped the place of private associations. Feelings and ideas are renewed, the heart enlarged, and the understanding developed only by the reciprocal action of men one upon another. I have shown how these influences are reduced almost to nothing in democratic countries; they must therefore be artificially created, and only associations can do that (Tocqueville 1969, 2: 515-16).

Tocqueville's understanding of the tyranny of the majority is tied to the natural equality that all citizens have, which provides them with the justification for the existence of their natural rights. As these rights were uncovered and practiced, political equality was demanded and received as a part of these rights. This encouraged a strident individualism that put citizens at increased risk of being tyrannized by the majority. For Tocqueville, associations stand as one of the most important impediments to tyranny of the majority.

Tocqueville's Corrections to the Tyranny of the Majority

For Tocqueville there are at least six ways in which the tyranny of the majority is tempered in America: the existence of free political association; a related freedom of civil association; newspapers and their ability to facilitate associations; the absence of administrative centralization; the counterbalancing effect of the American legal profession; and the jury as a political institution. Freedom of political association encourages citizens to combine intellectually in order to share their interests and advance their goals, assemble to formalize their influence, and pick leaders to present those ideas and goals in the political arena, where they had not previously been adequately represented due to majoritarian tyranny (Tocqueville 1969, 1:189-95, 2:520-24). Civil associations pave the way for political associations by teaching citizens to unite in their common interests in order to secure their individual freedom against the tyranny of the majority (1969, 2:513-17, 520-24). Newspapers act to reinforce associations by making many people aware of alternative points of view, and informing them of shared opinions that might encourage them to resist majoritarian tyranny (1969, 2:517-520). The absence of administrative centralization refers to the bureaucratic decentralization which acts as a safeguard against a tyrannical majority carrying out government policy unencumbered. The counterbalancing effect of the American legal profession relates to how lawyers have predilections toward aristocracy, which act as an impediment to the passions of democracy. The jury is understood by Tocqueville as a political institution that engenders a sense of duty, citizenship, and connectedness between the populace and its government, teaching the people about individual and minority rights under the law (1969, 1:262-276).

Tocqueville recognizes that association is used in America in a number of different ways. It is ingrained in citizens of the United States from birth that they must deal with the difficulties of life themselves, and that they should turn to authority in society only when they are unable to solve a problem without assistance. Even schoolchildren learn to abide by rules they establish in the games that they play. Associations are formed to eradicate local traffic problems, organize festivities, fight moral problems such as intemperance, provide for public security, support trade and industry, and further religious activity (1969, 1:189).

According to Tocqueville, political associations evolve through a three-stage process in order to become politically active. Once they become engaged in politics they can act to deter majoritarian oppression by offering alternatives to established law. In the first stage of the development of political associations, citizens can cooperate to demonstrate a shared intellectual interest in a particular doctrine. Tocqueville identifies this right as being similar to the freedom to write, but he believes political associations to be more powerful than the press. When political associations decide to present a point of view, they must be clearer and more precise than if they hadn't undertaken to formalize their ideas. Political associations identify supporters and draw them into the cause, increasing zeal and uniting the energies of "divergent minds" to work vigorously toward their goals (1969, 1:190).

The second stage involves freedom of assembly. Freedom of assembly allows diverse groups to increase their visibility and further their cohesiveness.

This stimulates activity throughout the country in places where the association seeks or has influence. Activities can be planned and built around the camaraderie engendered by members of the association being able to meet together. Tocqueville senses that the unity achieved by physically meeting and discussing opinions goes further in advancing interest in the associations' objectives than the written word could hope to accomplish (1969, 1:190).

The third and final stage involves the selection and use of political operatives to represent the views of the association. These operatives do not have the legal formal authority that elected representatives of the people have, but they can have influence on these government officials. The representatives of political associations cannot make the laws, but they can "attack existing laws" and suggest laws that would better serve their interests. Tocqueville likens these political associations and their operatives to a "separate nation within the nation and a government within the government" (1969, 1:190).

Tocqueville is cognizant of the threat that unlimited freedom of association may pose if groups seeking to overthrow the government organize to perpetrate violence against it. However, this danger must be weighed against the threat of majority tyranny. He states:

> In our own day freedom of association has become a necessary guarantee against the tyranny of the majority. In the United States, once a party has become predominant, all public power passes into its hands; its close supporters occupy all offices and have control of all organized forces. The most distinguished men of the opposite party, unable to cross the barrier keeping them from power, must be able to establish themselves outside it; the minority must use the whole of its moral authority to oppose the physical power oppressing it. The one danger has to be balanced against a more formidable one. The omnipotence of the majority seems to me such a danger to the American republics that the dangerous expedient used to curb it is actually something good (1969, 192).

Tocqueville insists that democratic states need free associations to hold back tyranny despite the threat that they may lead society to the verge of anarchy. Beyond protection from tyranny of the majority, free associations also discourage "secret societies." "There are factions in America," Tocqueville states, "but no conspirators" (1969, 193). He concludes, "Thus in the immense complication of human laws it sometimes comes about that extreme freedom corrects the abuse of freedom, and extreme democracy forestalls the dangers of democracy" (1969, 195).

Most associations in America are not political, but civil. Civil associations serve a variety of interests "which have no political object." They are "not only commercial and industrial associations," but "of a thousand different types." Civil associations can be "very general" or "very limited." They can be large or small and exist to do anything from building churches and distributing books to proclaiming a truth or propagating some feeling on a certain subject.

Despite his contention that civil associations make up the largest number of associations, it is asserted by Tocqueville that where "political associations are forbidden, civil associations are rare." Although common interests may cause people to share in many various undertakings that would encourage civil associations, rarely do these civil interests motivate great numbers to action, as political associations do. Tocqueville maintains that even if political associations don't exactly assist the progress or development of civil associations, to "destroy the former would harm the latter" (1969, 2:520-22). Civil associations can exist in a country where political associations are not allowed, but, as Tocqueville argues, "In such a country civil associations will always be few, feebly conceived, and unskillfully managed and either will never form any vast designs or will fail in the execution of them"(1969, 2:523).

The need for association in America stems from the weakening effect that equality has had on individuals. As citizens have become ever more equal, the powerful individuals of past aristocracies have not been available to wield the vast influences that they were once capable of wielding. Therefore, associations are necessary to "take the place of the powerful private persons whom equality of conditions has eliminated" (1969, 2:513-16). Tocqueville declares:

> Among laws controlling human societies there is one more precise and clearer, it seems to me, than all the others. If men are to remain civilized or to become civilized, the art of association must develop and improve among them at the same speed as equality of conditions spreads (1969, 2:517).

As the need for associations increases with the advance of equality, the importance of dispersing information about associations becomes paramount. In order to bring people together to cooperate in mutually shared concerns, it is necessary to inform them of commonly, or not so commonly, held opinions. Newspapers provide a necessary and essential connection between members of associations of all types and make other citizens aware of the interests and issues being brought forward by those associations. "Only a newspaper can put the same thought at the same time before a thousand readers" (Tocqueville 1969, 2:517).

As citizens labor to gain equality they are often caught up in their daily activities. Newspapers unite individuals by engaging them in public discourse in a way that doesn't distract them from their work. Liberty is protected by individuals being informed of associations that work to advance their common interests, but Tocqueville has determined that they do more than this (1969, 2:517). He states, "So the more equal men become and more individualism becomes a menace, the more necessary are newspapers. We should underrate their importance if we thought they just guaranteed liberty; they maintain civilization" (1969, 2: 517).

There is little doubt in Tocqueville's mind that newspapers can cause people to "do ill-considered things in common," but he holds that "they mend many more ills than they cause." Tocqueville believes that the "newspaper represents the association" by retrieving citizens from their isolated independence and speaking "to each of its readers in the name of all the rest " (1969, 2:517-18). He even supports a free press beyond an unlimited freedom of association. His assertion is that

> the more I observe the main effects of a free press, the more convinced am I that, in the modern world, freedom of the press is the principal and, so to say, the constitutive element in freedom. A nation bent on remaining free is therefore right to insist, at whatever cost, on respect for this freedom. But unlimited freedom of association must not be entirely identified with freedom to write. The former is both less necessary and more dangerous than the latter. A nation may set limits there without ceasing to be its own master; indeed in order to remain its own master, it is sometimes necessary to do so (1969, 1:191).

He concludes that in "America there is no limit to freedom of association for political ends," but the fatal results possible from this liberality have not come to pass because its use has become a part of "customs" and "mores" (1969, 1:191-92).

A fourth protection against the tyranny of the majority is bureaucratic decentralization. Tocqueville distinguishes between governmental and administrative centralization. He believes that there is governmental centralization because legislatures have near-total authority in the states, and that the national government is even more dominant (1969, 1:89-92). In fact, Tocqueville claims that the national government is centralized to the point that America is "more concentrated there than it ever was in any of the ancient European monarchies" (1969, 1:89). Governmental centralization creates a major threat of tyranny of the majority, but it is moderated by the absence of administrative centralization.

Tocqueville argues that administration is not centralized because the national government is occupied with larger issues and is not desirous of regulating society's secondary concerns. Also, it is impossible for the central government to force all citizens to respond to it in the same way simultaneously. The government simply does not have the administrative tools to compel this type of response. Furthermore, agents of the government carry out administration, and these agents cannot be controlled in every action they take at all times. These factors all act to mitigate the tyrannical threat of governmental centralization, but Tocqueville warns that if administrative centralization was ever condoned by the people and brought to fruition, it would be the worst type of despotism (1969, 1:262-63).

A fifth area that Tocqueville takes note of as a deterrent to the tyranny of the majority is the counterbalancing effect of the legal profession. He states that "men who have made a special study of the laws and have derived therefrom habits of order, something of a taste for formalities, and an instinctive love for a regular concatenation of ideas are naturally strongly opposed to the revolutionary spirit and to the ill-considered passions of democracy" (1969, 1:264).

Tocqueville sees lawyers as being like aristocrats without actually being aristocrats. The advantage here is that lawyers can mix their aristocratic distrust of unbridled democracy with their popularity among the people and act as a liaison between the people and the government (1969, 1:266).

Tocqueville may have put too much trust in lawyers by modern popular standards, but he believes that

> when the American people let themselves get intoxicated by their passions or carried away by their ideas, the lawyers apply an almost invisible brake which slows them down and halts them. Their aristocratic inclinations are secretly opposed to the instincts of democracy, their superstitious respect for all that is old to its love of novelty, their narrow views to its grandiose designs, their taste for formalities to its scorn of regulations, and their habit of advancing slowly to its impetuosity (1969, 1:268-69).

Tocqueville sees lawyers as positively influencing the desires of society in a way that restrains tyrannical majorities. He also identifies the exercise of judicial review as a tool to be wielded in the political arena if more restrained methods are ineffective (1969, 1:269). Judicial review has often worked to protect the minority. In the final analysis Tocqueville sees the law and politics as unavoidably intermixed. In his famous statement he concludes that, "There is hardly a political question in the United States which does not sooner or later turn into a judicial one" (1969, 1:270).

In keeping with trusting the legal side of American politics, Tocqueville defends the importance of the jury as a protection of minority rights. For Tocqueville the jury is not simply a judicial institution, it is a political institution. It is a political institution because it does more than affect the outcome of lawsuits. Juries engage the populace in its political process, thereby influencing "the fate of society" (1969, 1:272). Tocqueville thinks:

> Juries invest each citizen with a sort of magisterial office; they make all men feel that they have duties toward society and that they take a share in its government. By making men pay attention to things other than their own affairs, they combat that individual selfishness which is like rust in society (1969, 1: 274).

Juries place citizens in the position of having to judge their fellow man. Once put in the position to do this they can also see how they might be judged. This, Tocqueville argues, teaches the citizen equity. The greatest advantage that juries produce for society is that they are "wonderfully effective in shaping a nation's judgement and increasing its natural lights" (1969, 1:275).

Tocqueville indicates that civil juries are of particular importance in establishing a judicial way of thinking in citizens. He contends that civil court judges are more respected by jurors because they behave in a neutral, but instructive fashion. This is important because civil juries are formed from all classes of people, and their experience better prepares them to live in a free society. The responsibility of being a juror not only shows citizens that they rule in some fashion, but also it teaches them how to rule. The implication is that majorities will be tempered in their view and treatment of those with a minority position after serving on a jury (1969, 1:274-76).

One other protection to the tyranny of the majority could be identified, but only if Tocqueville had been clearer on the matter. Federalism appears to be both liked and disliked by Tocqueville (Schleifer 1980, 97). In a paragraph that is supportive of the federal system of government as an impediment to majority tyranny, Tocqueville makes this statement:

> As the Union's sovereignty is hampered and incomplete, its use is not at all dangerous to freedom. Moreover, it does not arouse that inordinate craving for power and renown which are so fatal to great republics. As there is no necessity for everything to end at one common center, one finds neither vast metropolises, nor immense wealth, nor extreme poverty, nor sudden revolutions. Political passions, instead of spreading like a sheet of fire instantaneously over the whole land, break up in conflict with individual passions of each state (1969, 1:162).

On the one hand, in an eerie prediction of conflict between the southern states and the Union, Tocqueville predicts passions will not be deterred by a federal system of government: "A man must have had very little experience of the ways of this world if he can imagine that, when a means has been left for the satisfaction of men's passions, they can always be prevented by legal fictions from seeing and using that means" (1969, 166).

Ralph C. Hancock is convinced that Tocqueville perceived American federalism as a combination of two goods: it provides the advantages of large and small-size nations. The states reflect a small nation where "they are concerned with the modest contentments of life, and they generally secure them." The Union is representative of large nations, where "there is more grandeur, more excitement, more intellectual stimulation, more progress." Whether any of this secures protection against tyranny of the majority is unclear (Hancock 1990, 91).

Tocqueville does agonize that there are not enough "guarantees against tyranny" in the United States. He wonders where one turns for protection against tyranny:

> When a man or a party suffers an injustice in the United States, to whom can he turn? To public opinion? That is what forms the majority. To the legislative body? It represents the majority and obeys it blindly. To the executive power? It is appointed by the majority and serves as its passive instrument. To the police? They are nothing but the majority under arms. A jury? The jury is the majority vested with the right to pronounce judgment; even the judges in certain states are elected by the majority. So however iniquitous or unreasonable the measure which hurts you, you must submit (1969, 252).

The protections against majority tyranny are not sufficient completely to satisfy Tocqueville. Something more is needed. I believe that Calhoun does have something additional to offer.

References

Allen, Barbara. 1991. "The Spiral of Silence & Institutional Design: Tocqueville's Analysis of Public Opinion & Democracy." *Polity*. Winter 1991. Vol. 24, No. 2:243-67.

Boesche, Roger. 1987. *The Strange Liberalism of Alexis de Tocqueville*. Ithaca, N.Y.: Cornell University Press.

Boesche, Roger. 1996. *Theories of Tyranny from Plato to Arendt*. University Park: The Pennsylvania State University Press.

Commager, Henry Steele. 1993. *Commager on Tocqueville*. Columbia: University of Missouri Press.

Lamberti, Jean-Claude. 1989. *Tocqueville and the Two Democracies*. Trans. Arthur Goldhammer. Cambridge, Mass.: Harvard University Press.

Hancock, Ralph C. 1990. "Tocqueville on the Good of American Federalism." *Publius: The Journal of Federalism*. Spring 1990. Vol. 20. No. 2:89-108.

Lively, Jack. 1965. *The Social and Political Thought of Alexis de Tocqueville*. Oxford: Clarendon Press.

Madison, James. With Alexander Hamilton, and John Jay. 1961. *The Federalist Papers*. Introduction by Clinton Rossiter. New York: New American Library.

Nelson, Brian R. 1996. *From Socrates to the Age of Ideology*. 2nd ed. Englewood Cliffs, N.J.: Prentice Hall.

Noelie-Neumann, Elisabeth. 1984. *The Spiral of Silence: Public Opinion—Our Social Skin*. Chicago: University of Chicago Press.

Roper, Jon. 1989. *Democracy and Its Critics: Anglo-American Democratic Thought in the Nineteenth Century*. London: Unwin Hyman.

Rossiter, Clinton. 1953. *Seedtime of the Republic: The Origin of the American Tradition of Political Liberty*. New York: Harcourt, Brace and Company.

Schleifer, James T. 1980. *The Making of Tocqueville's Democracy in America*. Chapel Hill: The University of North Carolina Press.

Tocqueville, Alexis de. 1969. *Democracy in America*. Trans. George Lawrence. Ed. J. P. Mayer. New York: Harper and Row.

Zetterbaum, Marvin. 1967. *Tocqueville and the Problem of Democracy*. Stanford, Calif.: Stanford University Press.

———. 1987. "Alexis De Tocqueville." *History of Political Philosophy*. 3rd ed. Ed. Leo Strauss and Joseph Cropsey. Chicago: University of Chicago Press.

Chapter 4

Calhoun

John Caldwell Calhoun was a planter, lawyer, statesman, and philosopher. He was active in public life for more than forty years at both the state and national levels—as a South Carolina legislator, a member of the U.S. House of Representatives, secretary of war, vice president, secretary of state, and U.S. senator. He also aspired to become President of the United States, but never attained that lofty goal. He served in national office at a time of increasing "sectional antagonisms," and became a primary spokesman for the "planter aristocracy of the South" (Spain 1951, 13).

Though Calhoun has been accused of being a slave to the issue of slavery; in fact, he was interested in and involved in a number of topics of the time that had nothing to do with slavery. He played an active part in banking, public land speculation, foreign policy unrelated to slavery, and was a keen observer of European political events. He did care for the Union, but it was his love of South Carolina and its economic dependence upon "agricultural capitalism" that led him to bring his considerable mental powers to the defense of slavery despite the high cost to his political aspirations of becoming president (Spain 1951, 30-33).

Calhoun knew what it was to pay the price of minority status. Calhoun was part of the nullification movement in South Carolina after the Tariff Acts of 1828 and 1832. Nullification was interconnected with the state-rights doctrine, which held that when the U.S. Constitution was ratified it put limits on the state governments, but not on the people from that state. That being the case, the people could call home their proxy when they deemed it necessary. The Tariff Acts caused South Carolina to deem it necessary, and it threatened secession (Calhoun 1953, introduction: xi-xviii; Bancroft 1966, 10-13, 117-26).

Tocqueville, who was aware of Calhoun's upholding nullification, was not favorable toward it. Tocqueville indicates that southern nullifiers would lead the United States back into the anarchy that existed before the Constitution was completed. While Tocqueville had concerns about democratic government becoming too centralized, he did not favor weakening the federal bond in the United States. Indeed, he thought that America would become weak because the Union was losing its grip (Tocqueville 1969, 389-95).

Nevertheless, powerful economic forces motivated Calhoun and others in the South to continue to support nullification and the possibility of secession. The Tariff Acts and South Carolina's threat to secede revolved around the economics of cotton, and slavery was directly connected to the production of cotton. It was a blatant oversight on the part of Calhoun not to see the connection between his minority status and that of slaves. Of course he did not see slaves as having the same status as himself, on a number of different levels, so he could easily rationalize their condition. Society grants rights, and slaves were not granted liberty for their own good. According to Calhoun, "Liberty, then, when forced on a people unfit for it, would, instead of a blessing, be a curse, as it would in its reaction lead directly to anarchy—the greatest of all curses. No people, indeed, can long enjoy more liberty than that to which their situation and advanced intelligence and morals fairly entitle them" (Calhoun 1953, 42).

By being unable to see the connection between his being tyrannized by the North and slaves' being tyrannized by whites, Calhoun was being consistent in upholding his belief that rights are granted as a part of a community agreement and not as a matter of natural rights. He did not consider slaves to be commensurate with white South Carolinians in their ability to be responsible about their liberty. South Carolina's citizens had been granted certain economic liberties, and it was their belief that some of those liberties had been seized from them. Slaves had never been granted liberty *ergo*, they were not having something taken away that they had been granted by society and the government.

While his defense of slavery was deplorable, Calhoun should not stand alone in being criticized for this defect. George Washington, Thomas Jefferson, and more directly related to this study, James Madison, owned slaves. Particularly with Madison, the ownership of slaves is at odds with his views on tyranny, especially when natural rights are invoked as a basis for the defense of minority interests. Calhoun does not support the notion of natural rights, and thereby escapes some of the hypocrisy associated with his defense of slavery. However, he does not correct for the inherent contradiction of believing southerners had been tyrannized by the majority in the North, while at the same time believing slaves had not been tyrannized because they had not earned the rights necessary to declare the harm they had suffered.

Despite Calhoun's apparent contradictions, he adds thought-provoking dimensions to the idea of the tyranny of the majority. He deplores the corruption that he perceives political parties wreak upon the process of governing in America by promoting tyrannical majorities. He provides a new correction to majoritarian tyranny with the notion of concurrent majorities, which would supply a form of interest representation that the U.S. Constitution does not contain. Calhoun's contradictions and contributions supply an alternative approach to the subject, one that is unique.

Calhoun's Tyranny of the Majority

John C. Calhoun determines that suffrage alone is not sufficient to protect the fundamental rights of minorities in a democratic constitutional government. Suffrage typically acknowledges only numerical majorities, or what he sometimes refers to as absolute majorities, which ignore other major interests that are not well represented by a majority voting system. According to Calhoun, with numerical majorities, "one regards numbers only and considers the whole community as a unit having but one common interest throughout, and collects the sense of the greater number of the whole as that of the community" (Calhoun 1953, 22).

Calhoun makes the case that when the majority is spoken of in political discourse, the numerical majority is what is meant, as though there were no alternative. The majority comes to be known as the entire people, and the government of the numerical majority comes to be known as the government of all, even though the government may rarely do what specific minorities would wish (Calhoun 1953, 19-25).

For Calhoun, numerical majorities are the method in which tyranny is brought about. As previously noted with Madison and Tocqueville, the tyranny of the majority originates with the people. Calhoun believes that it is man's nature to be more interested in his own well-being than that of others. Though men desire social interaction, their self-interestedness naturally puts them at odds with their fellow man. When men achieve the power of suffrage, they often use it to gain favor for their interests. Suffrage relies on quantitative measures to determine who is in authority, and the numerical majority becomes the so-called legitimate authority in democratic societies, often at the expense of the minority (Calhoun 1953, 3-25).

In addition to suffrage, the press and its ability to influence public opinion played an important part in promoting particular interests. While the press could be used to educate and inform the public, and could even assist in curtailing the threat of oppression and abuse of power, Calhoun feared that it to was being used mostly to promote selfish ends. He states two reasons why the press will be unable to counteract the ability of the numerical majority to abuse power or eliminate the need for some constitutional check on numerical majorities (Spain 1951, 113; Calhoun 1953, 56).

First, Calhoun believes that no matter how well the press does its job of increasing our knowledge and improving our understanding of each other, it won't change the part of nature, which makes constitutions necessary. The desire to control government is an eternal motivation for those seeking to promote their specific interests. Increased enlightenment about others' concerns will not alter the need to check constitutionally the numerical majority and keep it from abusing and oppressing the minority. The press may reduce the government's need to act, but it will not eliminate it (1953, 56-57).

Second, the press is very similar to suffrage. They are both expressions of public opinion. The press plays a larger part in the development of public opinion; suffrage is the authoritative expression of the public's opinion. The press will fail in expressing public opinion in the same way suffrage fails to do so; neither one of them expresses the opinion of the whole community. A constitutional check remains as necessary with a free press expressing its perception of public opinion as it does with suffrage (1953, 57-58). Calhoun states that

> what is called public opinion, instead of being the united opinion of the whole community, is usually nothing more than the opinion or voice of the strongest interest or combination of interests, and not unfrequently of a small but energetic and active portion of the whole. Public opinion, in relation to government and its policy, is as much divided and diversified as are the interests of the community; and the press, instead of being the organ of the whole, is usually but the organ of these various and diversified interests respectively, or rather of the parties growing out of them. It is used by them as the means of controlling public opinion and of so molding it as to promote their peculiar interests and to aid in carrying on the warfare of party. But as the organ and instrument of parties, in governments of the numerical majority, it is as incompetent as suffrage itself to counteract the tendency to oppression and abuse of power. (1953, 58).

Instead of diminishing threats of majoritarian tyranny, the press actually increases the intensity and the likelihood of its occurrence. By stirring up partisan conflicts the press actually increases the need for further constitutional checks. The struggle to control government becomes greater as the passions of public opinion are ignited by published reports of actual or perceived threats to guarded interests. The methods used to achieve that control become ever more oppressive. Once authority is established in the government, the government itself becomes an extension of that tyranny if it is not checked. The power granted those holding office in government is great. Even if communities were found that were completely equal in interests, the powers allotted to those running the government would be enough to divide the community by their decisions. Once the power of the government is won by a group that supports a particular interest, there is no equalizing that power with those who hold a different interest outside of government (Calhoun 1953, 14-16).

Calhoun also complains that unequal taxation and disbursement furthers majority influence in dominating the minority. If one group is taxed more than it receives back in disbursement, the government has split the community into two opposing sections, tax payers and tax consumers. Since the officials in power at the time are not likely to make those who elected them pay disproportionate taxes but are likely to disburse more in their direction, the minority is once again a probable target of majority oppression. As put in the case of *McCulloch v. Maryland,* the power to tax is the power to destroy. The community is divided between the ruling portion and the subject portion, and taxes are used in a system of rewards and punishments (Calhoun 1953, 16-19). Calhoun states:

Where the majority is that portion, it matters not how its powers may be exercised—whether directly by themselves or indirectly through representatives or agents. Be it which it may, the minority, for the time, will be as much the governed or subject portion as are the people in an aristocracy or the subjects in a monarchy. The only difference in this respect is that in the government of a majority the minority may become the majority, and the majority the minority, through the right of suffrage, and thereby change their relative positions without the intervention of force and revolution. But the duration or uncertainty of the tenure by which power is held cannot, of itself, counteract the tendency inherent in government to oppression and abuse of power. On the contrary, the very uncertainty of the tenure, combined with the violent party warfare which must ever precede a change of parties under such governments, would rather tend to increase than diminish the tendency to oppression (1953, 19).

The intermediary step of individuals joining political parties in order to have their interests represented must occur before there is adequate influence within the government to effect a tyranny of the majority. Parties often are indications of deeply held differences. Rather than settle these differences parties often inflame them. Parties carry out what is natural to man by pursuing their interests at the expense of other interests. It is the use of political parties by the majority to achieve individual interests that causes tyranny (Calhoun 1953, 19-25; Spain 1951, 108-17).

Calhoun understood that the ability of any individual voter to "protect his interest was subject to a number of limitations" (Spain 1951, 108). He was aware that compelling representatives to do what the voters wanted was precarious at best. Political parties were also created out of the necessity in representative government to connect representatives of the people with them in a way that would hopefully make them more accountable. The problem with parties is that they often become elaborate organizations that are ends unto themselves with powerful individual leaders that act from self-aggrandizement rather than the best interest of the country. It was for this reason that Calhoun did not support election by party ticket alone as opposed to election by individual candidacy. He feared that representative government overly influenced by party politics would turn into "machine politics and boss rule through party machinery" (109).

Patronage, or the spoils system, did become a function of party politics. Calhoun was anxious about its effects on party workers and voters. He feared that they would be willing to indulge any activity to gain favor and benefits. At worst, patronage "would sap the strength of patriotism, subvert liberty, and establish despotism (Spain 1951, 111).

Calhoun wanted to replace patronage with some form of merit system. He considered holding public office to be a public trust rather than slavish service to one's political party. As long as a public servant carried out his duty in an able and respectable manner he would be secure in his position. Permanence in public offices, as opposed to patronage, seemed a reasonable trade-off to Calhoun because it would limit party influence within the bureaucracy. If parties had less influence in the bureaucracy, that was one less opportunity for majorities to tyrannize minorities (Spain 1951, 111).

It was the absence of principle within the parties that tormented Calhoun. Too often real issues were clouded in the attempt to win elections in order that the party faithful could accrue the benefits that patronage would bring them. Also, the competition between the parties was becoming increasingly sharp in their wrangles for votes. Reckless promises and counterpromises were made in an inconsistent and contradictory manner. Any group could play the parties against one another to gain greater influence and increase the probability of achieving its objectives. Suffrage alone was becoming ever more unlikely to serve the purposes of good and fair representative government, because the parties were, seemingly, willing to win at the expense of those necessary virtues (Spain 1951, 110-12).

Parties, Calhoun asserts, were influenced by a number of different interests. If one interest did not predominate, those interests with the least difference would form a majority capable of being tyrannical. Separate interests were inspired by factors such as "similarity of origin, language, institutions, political tradition, customs, interests, color, . . . and geographical contiguity" (Spain 1951, 117). Geographical contiguity was considered by Calhoun to be the most powerful factor in initiating particular interests, because men "tended to sympathize with the familiar," and "interests were generally more similar within a given region" (117). The result was that "parties tended to become 'sectional' or 'local' in character and that majority oppression tended to become sectional exploitation" (Spain 1951, 117).

In a clear reference to tyranny of the North over the South, Calhoun predicts that a few powerful men in the hierarchy of the majority party, having been endowed with enormous powers in order to hold the party interests together, will tyrannize the "minority party or section, and leave them with no way to protect themselves, save revolution" (117). A change to something other than numerical majorities was necessary to avoid the travesty of parties becoming sectionalized. An addition to the government was needed that would allow all major interests a voice in their government.

Calhoun's Addition to the Definition of Tyranny

As with Tocqueville, the type of tyranny portrayed by Calhoun includes quantitative and qualitative elements. Calhoun identifies the quantitative element of suffrage as a primary culprit in producing numerical majorities. However, qualitative factors have frequently set in motion chains of events that resulted in numerical majorities. The qualitative elements of self-interest, a free press and public opinion, all contributed to or were intermingled with suffrage and numerical majorities in some way that results in majoritarian tyranny. Qualitative elements consistently act to influence quantitative elements (Roper 1989, 17).

Madison provided the concept of factions as a contributing qualitative element in establishing tyrannical majorities. Tocqueville expanded the number and the importance of qualitative elements in the creation of majority tyranny. Calhoun further extended the number of qualitative elements that can lead to majoritarian oppression. These new qualitative elements added by Calhoun stimulate the need for a new reconstruction of the definition of tyranny.

Calhoun, as with Tocqueville, does not directly define tyranny, or tyranny of the majority. What he does do is identify more qualitative elements that act as pathways to tyranny. The definition of tyranny in the last chapter took into account the qualifying effects that quantitative and qualitative elements had on the definition of tyranny. That definition focused on the destruction of natural rights by quantitative and qualitative elements. The constructed definition included the ideas of Madison, Dahl, Beahm, Fishkin, Roper, and Tocqueville. It stated, "Tyranny is every quantitative and qualitative destruction of a natural right, as determined to be a natural right by the people, with no serious objections."

Calhoun contributes an entirely differrent perspective from Madison and Tocqueville on how he might define tyranny, because he is clearly not a supporter of the idea of natural rights. Although Calhoun does write about the nature of man, he does not support the notion that man is born with natural rights that are bestowed upon him by a Creator and must be acknowledged by any government hoping to rule legitimately. Calhoun believes that all rights are granted by the community. It is only through the legitimate social and political authority that rights can be granted (Calhoun 1953, 40-45; Spain 1951, 85-89).

Taking Calhoun's view of rights into consideration, the definition of tyranny must be altered to reflect his contribution. If rights can be determined to be both natural rights and community-sanctioned rights, the definition should read as follows: "Tyranny is every quantitative and qualitative destruction of a right, as determined to be a right by the people, with no serious objections."

Also, to further clarify the definition of tyranny, "quantitative" and "qualitative" should be removed. They should be removed for two reasons. First, the term "quantitative" does not clearly indicate tyranny that may be initiated by a monarch, or tyrant, as the case may be; nor does it necessarily include tyranny caused by any form other than a majority. The term "qualitative" does not address the number of people who cause the tyranny, so it provides no meaningful assistance to the definition if the second reason for removing the two terms is understood and accepted. The second reason for removing "quantitative" and "qualitative" from the definition of tyranny is that if tyranny is considered to be every destruction of a right, then "quantitative" and "qualitative" must be understood to be included in every possible destruction of a right. Therefore, the definition of tyranny states, "Tyranny is every destruction of a right, as determined to be a right by the people, with no serious objections."

This definition of tyranny encompasses within it the very definition of all tyranny, including the definition of tyranny of the majority. All rights are also now included within this definition.

Calhoun's View of Rights

Calhoun does not support the concept of a social contract or natural rights, but he does defend the idea that man has a certain nature. He believes that the origin of government can be explained by understanding man's nature. In reverse, government also helps explain something about what man's nature is. Calhoun sets out to answer the following question: "What is that constitution or law of our nature without which government would not exist and with which its existence is necessary?" (Calhoun 1953, 3).

In order to answer this question Calhoun first assumes that it is an "incontestable fact that man is so constituted as to be a social being" (1953, 3). If man were not a social being he would not be driven to create government but would live mostly in isolation. The fact that man is a social being requires that government be in place to cope with the problems of his social existence. Calhoun states:

> His inclinations and wants, physical and moral, irresistibly impel him to associate with his kind; and he has, accordingly, never been found, in any age or country, in any state other than the social. In no other, indeed, could he exist, and in no other—were it possible for him to exist—could he attain to a full development of his moral and intellectual faculties or raise himself, in the scale of being, much above the level of the brute creation (1953, 3).

Calhoun's second assumption contends that it is also an incontestable fact that "while man is so constituted as to make the social state necessaary to his existence and the full development of his faculties, this state itself cannot exist without government" (1953, 3). Man is by nature a social being. The social state aids man's existence and his development as a social being. Government facilitates the social state necessary for man to be his most complete social self.

Convinced that he has answered the first question, Calhoun moves on to state the following primary and important question, "What is that constitution of our nature which, while it impels man to associate with his kind, renders it impossible for society to exist without government?" (1953, 4).

Calhoun responds to the question by stating:

> The answer will be found in the fact (not less incontestable than either of the others) that while man is created for the social state and is accordingly so formed as to feel what affects others as well as what affects himself, he is, at the same time, so constituted as to feel more intensely what affects him directly than what affects him indirectly through others, or, to express it differently, he is so constituted that his direct or individual affections are stronger than his sympathetic or social feelings. I intentionally avoid the expression "selfish feelings" as applicable to the former, because, as commonly used, it implies an unusual excess of the individual over the social feelings in the person to whom it is applied and, consequently, something depraved and vicious.

My object is to exclude such inference and to restrict the inquiry exclusively to facts in their hearings on the subject under consideration, viewed as mere phenomena appertaining to our nature—constituted as it is; and which are as unquestionable as is that of gravitation or any other phenomenon of the material world (1953, 4).

Calhoun does not deny that there are times when special relations or circumstances compel people to consider others over themselves. However, these occurrences he understands to be "something extraordinary." They are demonstrated to be extraordinary by the "deep impression" that is left by the act or event. Calhoun thinks the attention paid to these acts of self-sacrifice is proof in themselves that they should be treated as an exception "to some general and well-understood law of our nature" (1953, 4).

Calhoun maintains that this "law of our nature" is "essentially connected with the great law of self-preservation which pervades all that feels." This phenomenon of self-preservation is found nowhere to be stronger than it is in man. Despite man's social feelings, intellect, and morality he still is not able to "overcome this all-pervading and essential law of animated existence" (1953, 5). Like Thomas Hobbes (1962), Calhoun deems self-preservation and self-interest to be man's primary concern. It is from this attention to self that conflict between individuals arises. Each person, having greater regard for his well-being than that of others, will come into conflict with those who have opposing interests. These conflicting interests will be further fueled by the passions of "suspicion, jealousy, anger, and revenge." These passions will ignite acts of "insolence, fraud, and cruelty," which if not deterred by some "controlling power" will end in chaos leading to the destruction of the "social state." "This controlling power, wherever vested or by whomsoever exercised, is Government" (Calhoun 1953, 5). Calhoun holds that

it follows, then, that man is so constituted that government is necessary to the existence of society, and society to his existence and the perfection of his faculties. It follows also that government has its origin in this twofold constitution of his nature: the sympathetic or social feelings constituting the remote, and the individual or direct the proximate, cause (1953, 5).

For Calhoun society and government are intertwined, but society is "first in the order of things" and the greater of the two. Society is primary because its preserves and perfects "our race." Government is "secondary and subordinate" to society because it preserves and perfects society. Government could have been forgone if man had been less of a social being, or if he had cared at least equally, if not more, for his fellow man than himself. Neither of these is possible, to Calhoun's way of thinking, so government becomes necessary to the well being of man (1953, 5-6).

Calhoun does contemplate what society would be like if individuals cared as much, or more, for others than themselves. He predicts that all individuality would be lost and "remediless disorder and confusion would ensue." Each person would be so caught up in the affairs of others that he would not be able to manage his own. This arrangement would lead to such upheaval that the result would be "not less destructive to our race than a state of anarchy." If government were possible at all, its object would have to be reversed (1953, 6). He speculates that

> selfishness would have to be encouraged, and benevolence discouraged. Individuals would have to be encouraged by rewards to become more selfish, and deterred by punishments from being too benevolent; and this, too, by a government administered by those who, on the supposition, would have the greatest aversion for selfishness and the highest admiration for benevolence (1953, 6-7).

Calhoun does give credit to the "Creator" for ordering man's nature in such a way that his capabilities match his condition. In his doing so I find that Calhoun is very careful to not slide off into the abyss of social-contractarian natural-rights jargon when referring to the role that the "Infinite Being" has assigned to his creations (1953, 7). Calhoun states:

> He, in his infinite wisdom and goodness, has allotted to every class of animated beings its condition and appropriate functions and has endowed each with feelings, instincts, capacities, and faculties best adapted to its allotted condition(1953, 7).

This characterization of the Creator's will reflects a logical ordering of all living things. It is also an empirical part of Calhoun's defense of slavery. Men are endowed with unequal abilities, and Calhoun argues that the Creator has provided particular social and political states to fit them. He declares:

> To man, he has assigned the social and political state as best adapted to develop the great capacities and faculties, intellectual and moral, with which he has endowed him, and has, accordingly, constituted him so as not only to impel him into the social state, but to make government necessary for his preservation and well-being (1953, 7).

Calhoun rejects the traditional theory of "natural liberty and equality of all men." With this rejection he clearly abandons many of the tenets laid down in the Declaration of Independence. Men are not born free; they are brought into a world of subjection where their elders are in control, and as they age there is always someone with whom they must contend. Men are not equal, because of differing capabilities between them. Even the same person is not equal to himself during different periods of his life. A person progresses through different stages, gaining knowledge and improving his talents throughout his life. A child generally doesn't know and can't do what the same person as an adult does. Therefore, the assumptions of the natural law doctrine were not a legitimate claim to natural rights for Calhoun (Calhoun 1953, 43-45; Spain 1951, 85-89).

I believe that rights for Calhoun were those that were sanctioned by the community. He believed that man had a certain nature that was determined by the Creator, but this did not mean that the Creator had granted natural rights to man. It was man's nature to be both a social being and yet be more concerned with his own well-being. It was the government's job, through the citizens, to determine which rights would be granted to which people in the society. Calhoun believed this was the way rights had historically been granted, and that it had been done this way because there was no other authority that could grant rights. The Creator had given man a certain nature; now it was up to man to determine which rights he and his fellow citizens were capable of handling. It was apparent to Calhoun that some men were more capable of handling certain rights than others. If the Creator had truly created all men equal, they would all have the same rights, which could be called natural rights. Calhoun thought it clear that all men were not equal, therefore natural rights couldn't be assumed (Spain 1951, 85-90).

Calhoun thought the doctrines of natural rights were destructive of "social order and safety." Government could not be constructed properly if anarchical principles of natural rights were applied. Calhoun believed that the ideas and practices which supported natural rights doctrines were rushing the U.S. into an untested social condition. He blamed abolitionists for promoting natural rights at the expense of southern institutions (Spain 1951, 90-91).

Even though Calhoun was convinced that southern institutions were under siege by abolitionists, he thought northerners should be concerned about their capitalist endeavors. If natural rights and the ideal of equality are taken to their logical conclusion, all property rights are threatened. The industrial capitalists of the North were probably more at risk than the agrarian capitalists of the South because of their disproportional wealth (Spain 1951, 91). Spain indicates of Calhoun that "his estimate of the immediacy of the danger was somewhat askew, but he was followed by writers of a different cast in his belief that the logical conclusion of the democratic ideal was socialism" (1951, 91).

In challenging the ideas of social contract theory, equality, and natural rights, Calhoun was carving a new path in American political thought. He did so by challenging the logical and historical soundness of these ideas. I maintain that Calhoun's thought was much more in keeping with the Aristotelian order of political relationships than had been readily accepted in America (Aristotle 1978). Unquestionably, Calhoun's challenge to social contract theory and the entire realm of natural rights was done in the recognition that these ideas were inconsistent with slavery (Spain 1951, 91-92).

Rights are not bestowed on man by his Creator, according to Calhoun; they are sanctioned by the community through their legitimate authority, or government. It would seem reasonable that if the community sanctions rights it also would have the right to take them away by a legitimate process—a prospect Calhoun does not adequately address. He does understand that government can do harm to people because government is made up of people who are self-interested. If enough people of the same interest choose to tyrannize over others who hold contrary points of view, government can be used as a tool to damage or even destroy those in the minority. Calhoun's conception of man's nature allows for the possibility that tyrannical majorities will exist. That is why constitutions are necessary—to provide for protections against self-interested majorities that govern at the expense of the minority.

Calhoun's Corrections to the Tyranny of the Majority

Calhoun recognizes that history is rife with examples of government abusing its power. This abuse is a result of the self-interest that makes government necessary to begin with. He maintains that

> the powers which it is necessary for government to possess in order to repress violence and preserve order cannot execute themselves. They must be administered by men in whom, like others, the individual are stronger than the social feelings. And hence the powers vested in them to prevent injustice and oppression on the part of others will, if left unguarded, be by them converted into instruments to oppress the rest of the community. That by which this is prevented, by whatever name called, is what is meant by constitution, in its most comprehensive sense, when applied to government. Having its origin in the same principle of our nature, constitution stands to government as government stands to society; and as the end for which society is ordained would be defeated without government, so that for which government is ordained would, in a great measure, be defeated without constitution (1953, 7).

Calhoun does think that constitutions differ from government in two significant ways. First, necessity forces government to exist. Constitutions, on the other hand, are extremely difficult to construct so that they do their required job of counteracting governmental tendencies toward "oppression and abuse." Second, constitutions are the "contrivance of man," but government is a "divine ordination." "Man is left to perfect what the wisdom of the Infinite ordained as necessary to preserve the race" (1953, 8). Being left to perfect constitutions that will prevent government from being used for self-aggrandizement, Calhoun considers two alternatives. He rejects the notion that a higher authority than government could be put in place, because it would simply become the new government and would suffer from the same faults. He also rejects reducing the amount of power the government has, because it would then become "too feeble to protect and preserve society." What is of first and foremost importance in constructing a constitutional government is suffrage (1953, 10-11). Calhoun states:

> Such an organism, then, as will furnish the means by which resistance may be systematically and peaceably made on the part of the ruled to oppression and abuse of power on the part of the rulers is the first and indispensable step toward forming a constitutional government. And as this can only be effected by

or through the right of suffrage—the right on the part of the ruled to choose their rulers at proper intervals and to hold them thereby responsible for their conduct—the responsibility of the rulers to the ruled, through the right of suffrage, is the indispensable and primary principle in the foundation of a constitutional government. When this right is properly guarded, and the people sufficiently enlightened to understand their own rights and the interests of the community and duly to appreciate the motives and conduct of those appointed to make and execute the laws, it is all-sufficient to give to those who elect effective control over those they have elected (1953, 11).

Suffrage acts to deter oppression or tyranny by making government officials accountable to the governed. While suffrage deters one form of oppression it creates another by transferring power to the community, essentially making them the rulers. Calhoun considers that

the sum total, then, of its effects, when most successful, is to make those elected the true and faithful representatives of those who elected them—instead of irresponsible rulers, as they would be without it; and thus, by converting it into an agency, and the rulers into agents, to divest government of all claims to sovereignty and to retain it unimpaired to the community. But it is manifest that the right of suffrage in making these changes transfers, in reality, the actual control over the government from those who make and execute the laws to the body of the community and thereby places the powers of the government as fully in the mass of the community as they would be if they, in fact, had assembled, made, and executed the laws themselves without the intervention of representatives or agents. The more perfectly it does this, the more perfectly it accomplishes its ends; but in doing so, it only changes the seat of authority without counteracting, in the least the tendency of the government to oppression and abuse of its powers (1953, 12-13).

Suffrage solves the problem of unelected rulers abusing their authority but creates the new problem of the public becoming the new potential oppressor. Particular interests form in the community to protect their concerns (Madison referred to them as factions), and they elect officials to office who will support their interests. If no one interest is strong enough to sway political officials to back its positions, then interests will unite that have common goals in order to achieve their objectives. The result will inevitably be a split in the community by the generation of a major and minor party (Calhoun 1953, 13-14).

Parties reinforce and perpetuate dominance by numerical majorities through the use of suffrage. Parties do not cancel out competing interests but work to unite them, increasing their power. Parties that support minority interests are at a distinct disadvantage in gaining any leverage to support their concerns. Minority interests need to have a way of being represented within the government such that strict majoritarian will is not always the controlling factor (Spain 1951, 108-17).

Since Calhoun believes that numerical majorities, or absolute majorities, contribute to minorities being tyrannized, it is his contention that something beyond suffrage is needed to counteract the threat of majoritarian tyranny. The countermeasure he proposes is referred to as "concurrent majorities," or "constitutional majorities." Concurrent majorities

> regards interests as well as numbers—considering the community as made up of different and conflicting interests, as far as the action of the government is concerned—and takes the sense of each through its majority or appropriate organ, and the united sense of all as the sense of the entire community (Calhoun 1953, 23).

Calhoun is arguing for an organism of the government that will allow those who are not a part of the numerical majority to be protected from its overbearing power. Calhoun states:

> It follows that the two, suffrage and proper organism combined, are sufficient to counteract the tendency of government to oppression and abuse of power and to restrict it to the fulfillment of the great ends for which it is ordained" (Calhoun 1953, 21).

The organism that will provide for concurrent majorities will be a governmental apparatus in which societal interests that are frequently treated unfairly by the government will have an opportunity to concur in or veto decisions made by the government (Calhoun 1953, 19-21). The positive power is what allows government to act. This would simply be a numerical majority vote confirming a decision. The negative power of the organism would stop the government from action. This negative power could be provided through a "veto, interposition, nullification, check, or balance of power" (28). Calhoun is convinced that the negative power is necessary to prevent the minority from being oppressed by the majority. Constitutions require both positive and negative powers to be able to act, and to prevent actions from occurring. Concurrent majorities are a necessary counterbalance to the strict numerical majorities, which if allowed to stand alone would ultimately lead to absolute government (28).

What Calhoun has added to the protections against the tyranny of the majority goes beyond what Madison and Tocqueville suggested; it adds the concept of interest representation. Calhoun wants particular groups that suffer consistently from majority oppression to have an alternative constitutional power that will offer them some protection where they are not now protected. Concurrent majorities would offer that protection by asking disaffected groups to concur with decisions made by the government that would affect them. If a group did not concur, its action would have the effect of a veto. Calhoun believes concurrence would work like a jury (1953, 50-51).

Trial by jury puts a dozen people together to resolve conflicts that have been unsettled up to that point in time. Despite doubts about this method it is exceptionally effective. Calhoun believes that juries come to unanimous verdicts out of the need to have the matter decided. He is convinced that this would be the case in the political world as long as the conflicts had some degree of urgency. He states:

> Nothing, indeed, can be more favorable to the success of truth and justice than this predisposing influence caused by the necessity of being unanimous. It is so much so as to compensate for the defect of legal knowledge and a high degree of intelligence on the part of those who usually compose juries. If the necessity of unanimity were dispensed with and the finding of a jury made to depend on a bare majority, jury trial, instead of being one of the greatest improvements in the judicial department of government, would be one of the greatest evils that could be inflicted on the community. It would be, in such case, the conduit through which all the factious feelings of the day would enter and contaminate justice at its source (1953, 51).

John L. Safford suggests concurrence would resemble the operations of the Security Council of the United Nations, where permanent members have a veto on the use of coercion (1995, 212).

Calhoun understood that to make democratic government work, compromise would be necessary. The use of concurrent majorities would compel individuals to compromise in order to avoid harm to those who could not protect their interests through majoritarian practices. Calhoun thought that promoting the common good included giving every part of the citizenry a chance to protect its interests. He states that:

> to enlist the individual on the side of the social feelings to promote the good of the whole is the greatest possible achievement of the science of government, while to enlist the social on the side of the individual to promote the interest of parties at the expense of the good of the whole is the greatest blunder which ignorance can possibly commit" (1953, 53).

Calhoun has widely been criticized for his failure to include blacks as a part of the citizenry. Despite this blind spot I believe that Calhoun managed to construct logically one of the soundest theories on the tyranny of the majority of any author on the subject. His ideas about concurrent majorities and how they support the notion of interest representation was and is groundbreaking work. As will be discussed in the next chapter, Lani Guinier, in her book *The Tyranny of the Majority*, makes arguments similar to Calhoun's on the subject of interest representation. As Safford has stated, "Calhoun perverted the practice of concurrent majority by excluding blacks from voting. That alone, however, doesn't invalidate the minority veto as a democratic means of dealing with extreme or otherwise irreconcilable cases of majority tyranny" (1995, 216).

If Lani Guinier, a black female in the latter part of the twentieth-century, can discern truth in an idea of John C. Calhoun, a nineteenth-century slave owner, then alternative conceptions of the tyranny of the majority do not seem so far apart.

Notes

Nullification is defined as the alleged right of a state of the Union to declare an act of Congress inapplicable, null and void, and without force or effect, within its own borders (Calhoun 1953, xi, note 6).

References

Aristotle. 1978. *The Politics of Aristotle*. London: Oxford University Press.

Bancroft, Frederic. 1966. *Calhoun and the South Carolina Nullification Movement*. Gloucester: Peter Smith.

Calhoun, John C. 1953. *A Disquisition on Government and Selections on the Discourse*. New York: Liberal Arts Press.

Dahl, Robert A. 1956. *A Preface to Democratic Theory*. Chicago: University of Chicago Press.

Fishkin, James S. 1979. *Tyranny and Legitimacy: A Critique of Political Theories*. Baltimore: Johns Hopkins University Press.

Hobbes, Thomas. 1962. *Leviathan*. Ed. Michael Oakeshott. Introduction by Richard S. Peters. New York: Collier Books.

Madison, James. With Alexander Hamilton and John Jay. 1961. *The Federalist Papers*. Introduction by Clinton Rossiter. New York: New American Library.

McCulloch v. Maryland. 4 Wheat 316 (1819).

Roper, Jon. 1989. *Democracy and Its Critics: Anglo-American Democratic Thought in the Nineteenth Century*. London: Unwin Hyman.

Safford, John L. 1995. "John C. Calhoun, Lani Guinier, and Minority Rights." *Political Science* 26 (2): 211-16.

Spain, August O. 1951. *The Political Theory of John C. Calhoun*. New York: Bookman Associates.

Tocqueville, Alexis de. 1969. *Democracy in America*. Trans. George Lawrence. Ed. J. P. Mayer. New York: Harper and Row.

Chapter 5

Dahl and Guinier

Robert A. Dahl and Lani Guinier represent two distinct modern conceptualizations of the tyranny of the majority. Dahl is a distinguished political theorist whose contribution to democratic theory in the latter half of the twentieth Century cannot be exaggerated. His book *A Preface to Democratic Theory* stands as one of the premier works on how popular sovereignty functions in America's democratic republic. To ignore his views on the subject of the tyranny of the majority would be a grave loss to any evaluation of the topic, despite the fact that he finds the danger of majoritarian tyranny to be inflated beyond its true importance. Dahl believes that equality should be maximized because it provides for fair representation of people's interests. He does not like checks and balances because they give too much authority to minorities, both in the public, and in the government. The increased authority allotted to minorities through constitutional checks does damage to the concepts of procedural democracy and equality. Since theories of the tyranny of the majority rely on checks against oppressive majorities, Dahl finds them contrary to representative democracy (Dahl 1956; Dahl 1996). For his contribution on this subject, Dahl deserves a serious examination and response.

Lani Guinier is an accomplished civil rights lawyer who achieved a status in her profession commensurate with being appointed by President Bill Clinton as the assistant attorney general of the Civil Rights Division of the Justice Department. The appointment was withdrawn after a wave of complaints from her critics that she favored a "racial spoils system." She was never allowed the opportunity to air her views in a public hearing (Guinier 1994, vii). She responded to her critics, and the indignity of not being given the opportunity to be heard, by writing *The Tyranny of the Majority*. She has since published a new book on civil rights and social justice entitled *Lift Every Voice*.

Guinier contributed to the discussion on the tyranny of the majority in her first book by clarifying how blacks have been marginalized by America's version of representative democracy. She writes from the authoritative position of understanding what it is to be in a distinct minority, while simultaneously comprehending the legal/historical factors that have led to the treatment that this group has endured. Her analysis of voting in America provides a perspective on its effects that suggests some alternative voting scheme may be necessary. She not only believes that tyranny of the majority exists against blacks but that it has become entrenched by the system of popular sovereignty in America.

Dahl and Guinier epitomize the modern dichotomy in the debate over majority tyranny. Dahl doubts that the problem even exists; Guinier thinks that the problem is intractable under the current voting arrangement. Dahl raises important questions about the viability of a theory of the tyranny of the majority; Guinier suggests alternatives to the current voting practices in America that she believes will limit the effect of the tyranny of the majority. The following discourse attempts to clarify their positions.

Dahl's Argument against a Theory of the Tyranny of the Majority

Robert A. Dahl is one of the most forceful critics of the alternative conceptions of the tyranny of the majority (1956, 4-34, 133; 1985, 7-51; 1989, 169-73). His argument against different conceptions of the tyranny of the majority is based on the belief that majorities do not rule, only minorities rule. The idea of minority rule comes from a number of different sources. Three will be utilized to demonstrate Dahl's position.

First, Dahl paraphrases the idea of minority rule as put by Gaetano Mosca that societies develop a ruling class, and that the ruling class is never the majority because the ruling class will never allow the majority to seize power. In fact, Mosca argues that societies living under the pretense of majority rule are the most likely to be tyrannized because the ruling class will "claim to represent the majority," legitimizing their decisions and their hold on power (1956, 54-55). *Ergo*, only minority tyranny is possible if majorities don't rule.

Somewhat surprisingly, Madison is a second source of the idea of minority rule. Even he agrees that a majority faction in a large democratic republic is not likely to dominate. He states:

> Extend the sphere and you take in a greater variety of parties and interests; you make it less probable that a majority of the whole will have a common motive to invade the rights of other citizens; or if such a common motive exists, it will be more difficult for all who feel it to discover their own strength and to act in unison with each other" (Madison 1961, *Federalist 10:*83).

Of course, Madison thought there should be protections against majority tyranny set up within the government if varied parties and interests didn't prevent it, but he believed that competing factions would limit the chances of an over-bearing majority seizing control (1961, *Federalist 10:*77-84).

The idea of minority rule can also be defended by the empirical evidence of recent presidential and congressional elections in America. Roughly, only half of the voters who could register and vote in presidential elections actually do vote. In off-year congressional elections turnout is even worse (Peterson 1963; Scammon 1991; Piven and Cloward 1988). If at best only half of the eligible population is voting, even a majority victory means that a minority is ruling by way of the vote.

What Dahl proposes, in response to his belief that minorities rule, is a polyarchal theory of democracy that takes into account the two different methodological approaches of maximization and description. The maximization method proposes to maximize Madisonian principles, such as a "non-tyrannical republic," or, populistic notions, such as popular sovereignty and political equality. The descriptive method considers phenomena associated with democratic nations and social organizations in an attempt to identify distinguishing characteristics they have in common, and to consider "the necessary and sufficient conditions for social organizations possessing these characteristics" (1956, 63). Dahl finds that it is necessary to combine both the maximization and the descriptive method to produce an adequate democratic theory. While applying the descriptive method, he chooses to concentrate on the populistic theory of political equality, suggested by the maximization method. He does not reject the principle of a nontyrannical republic, but he does disagree with Madison on whether minorities need special protection from majority tyranny since minorities rule (1956, 63-85). Dahl's sentiment on the whole issue of majority tyranny is reasonably summarized in his statement that "if majority rule is mostly a myth, then majority tyranny is mostly a myth too. For if the majority cannot rule, surely it cannot be tyrannical" (Dahl 1956, 133).

Polyarchy relies on social checks and balances to protect both the majorities and minorities, rather than constitutional checks that mostly restrain majorities. Dahl identifies these social checks and balances as societal norms that people are taught and pressured to abide by (through their conscience), when there is broad agreement on what they are (1956, 22, 36, 81-83). He states, "As distinguished from Madisonianism, the theory of polyarchy focuses primarily not on the constitutional prerequisites but on the social prerequisites for a democratic order" (1956, 82).

Dahl is more concerned with society building than he is with constitution building. He believes that if the groundwork for constructing society is not firm, a constitutionally based government cannot be expected to work well either. He contends:

> We admire the efficacy of constitutional separation of powers in curbing majorities and minorities, but we often ignore the importance of the restraints imposed by the social separation of powers. Yet if the theory of polyarchy is roughly sound, it follows that in the absence of certain social prerequisites, no

constitutional arrangements can produce a non-tyrannical republic. The history of numerous Latin-American states. is, I think, sufficient evidence. Conversely, an increase in the extent to which one of the social prerequisites is present may be far more important in strengthening democracy than any particular constitutional design. Whether we are concerned with tyranny by a minority or tyranny by a majority, the theory of polyarch suggest that the first and crucial variables to which political scientists must direct their attention are social and not constitutional (1956, 83).

It is the attention to constitution building and its affect on the democratic process that Dahl finds troubling about Madisonianism. Dahl concludes his first chapter of *A Preface to Democratic Theory* by explaining how Madison constructs two irreconcilable goals. One is that citizens, having equal rights, are included in determining the general direction of government policy. The second goal that Dahl attributes to Madison is that majorities had to be "constitutionally inhibited." Since these two goals are conflicting, Dahl suggests that only one of the two be selected for further advancement (1956, 32-33). The latter of the two goals he believes is the product of an "antidemocratic" theory, and has been shared "not only by aristocratic elites but also by political adventurers, fanatics, and totalitarians of all kinds, so that this style of thought takes many forms and finds advocates as different as Plato and Lenin" (Dahl 1956, 31-32). Dahl believes that it goes a bit too far to characterize Madison's theory as being contrary to democracy. Nonetheless, that is the inference that he draws.

The goal that Dahl chooses to pursue is the maximization of political equality (1956, 63-85; 1996, 639-48). This is a reasonable choice in light of his depiction of Madison's theory of the tyranny of the majority. The problem with Dahl's choice is this: Can one maximize political equality and still protect minority rights? If everyone is equal in determining government policies, the majority, when there is one, or perhaps even a plurality, will have at least the opportunity to violate the rights of the minority. Dahl does not say that majorities never rule; he says that "if majority rule is mostly a myth, then majority tyranny is mostly a myth too" (1956, 133). In an interesting statement meant to support the democratic process, Dahl states, "There is, I believe, no case on record where a persistent law-making majority has not, sooner or later, achieved its purposes" (1956, 110).

This is at least tacit acknowledgment that majorities do dominate at times. As Madison has shown, it is possible to avoid unnecessarily trammeling upon the rights of the minority, but it requires safeguarding the minority from the overbearing nature of the majority (Madison 1961, *Federalist 51*:320).

Dahl thinks that minorities will be treated fairly if equality is maximized within the democratic process. Madison believes that equality can be maximized in the democratic process only if minorities are granted special constitutional protections. Obviously Dahl is concerned that constitutional inhibitions end up elevating minorities to the status of an elite, who would determine what was "inherently right or good" (Dahl 1956, 31). Although his fear is understandable, the perception of right and good has often been proclaimed through democratic processes before, and some of these results also produced totalitarianism (Talmon 1970).

To Dahl's credit, he does not think that minority rights can be violated without violating the tenets of a democratic society (Dahl 1989, 171). In his book *Democracy and Its Critics*, Dahl proceeds with a discussion between an "Advocate" of procedural democracy and a "Critic" who believes procedural democracy puts substantive interests at risk. Dahl assumes the role of the Advocate in this mock discussion. The result is an intriguing exchange between the two that helps to clarify Dahl's position on majority tyranny. Probably the most telling comments from the Advocate about protection of minority rights are expressed as follows:

> In a stable democracy a commitment to the protection of all the primary political rights would become an essential element of the political culture, particularly as that culture was borne, interpreted, and transmitted by persons bearing a special responsibility for the interpretation and enforcement of rights—as jurists do,.for example. Unless the democratic process and the primary political rights necessary to it were supported in this way by the political culture of a people, it's unlikely that the democratic process would persist. . . . When the democratic process can no longer be sustained in the face of a weak or hostile political culture, it strains credulity to believe that primary political rights will be preserved for long by courts or any other institution (Dahl 1989, 172-73).

Dahl's case that the democratic process cannot be maintained in a hostile political culture is a convincing one. However, this view takes a worst-case-scenario approach. Not every violation of minority rights, although troublesome, is evidence that the political culture is breaking down. Even if it were, constitutional checks can often act to prevent a further collapse. Frequently the Senate, the president, or the courts have acted to preserve primary political rights. Oddly, Dahl overestimates the negative effect of a limited number of cases where minority rights are threatened, but perhaps he does this with the consideration that constitutional checks would not be available in the democratic society he constructs.

Dahl's Addition to the Definition of Tyranny

Dahl does not provide a definition of tyranny, or of the tyranny of the majority, except to reconstruct and critique Madison's and Fishkin's definitions (Dahl 1956; 4-33; 1985, 15-16; Fishkin 1979). Dahl characterizes Madison's definition of tyranny as "every severe deprivation of a natural right" (Dahl 1956, 6). This characterization of Madison's definition does identify important factors considered by Madison in arriving at his use of the word tyranny. However, "severe deprivation" and "natural right" are phrases inserted by Dahl to provide what he believes to be a fuller rendering of the definition of tyranny. The problem is that Dahl does not fully explain how he understands these terms either.

Dahl is correct to assert that Madison's definition of tyranny is arbitrary, but the characterization of Madison's definition leaves room for improvement as well. Dahl confesses that it is a "little unfair to treat Madison as a political theorist," since Madison's writings were so politically charged and motivated (Dahl 1956, 5). Agreed. Then why not simply say that Madison did not define tyranny sufficiently and proceed with the business of doing so? The answer for Dahl is that he does not believe that tyranny can be defined in a fashion that is "consistent with and necessary to the argument" of Madison's system as a whole (Dahl 1956, 24). Part of the difficulty is that Madison was not attempting to define tyranny in the context of a complete political theory, as Dahl recognizes. Moreover, Dahl looks at Madison's attempt at defining tyranny in near-complete isolation from his other writings.

Dahl also critiques Fishkin's definition of tyranny and finds it wanting (Dahl 1985, 15). In Dahl's *A Preface to Economic Democracy*, Fishkin's discussion of "essential interests" (see chapter 2) is invoked to look at a narrowed definition of tyranny, and also to demonstrate that in some situations government policy will lead to "either injustice or tyranny" no matter what it does (15-16). The example that Dahl uses is as follows:

> If child labor is in some circumstances unjust; and if it is an essential interest of employers to hire children; and if existing laws protect the legal right of employers to hire children: then either child labor cannot be legally forbidden, which would be unjust, or by forbidding it government must necessarily act tyrannically" (1985, 15).

Fishkin would have government avoid tyranny where possible. However, he contends that only the most "horrendous" and severe deprivations that destroy essential interests should be avoided, when both parties are at risk of being damaged (Fishkin 1979, 19). In this case, it is difficult to raise concern for the destruction of the essential interest of an employer above the injustice that might be done by hiring children. Checks imposed in situations like this, where litigation of the issue is likely, may not be the most democratic way to proceed, but it may be the most just.

If there is anything that Dahl could add to the definition of tyranny, I believe it would have to deal with the violation or the destruction of the democratic process. Dahl lists five criteria that are necessary for a democratic process. They are: equal votes, effective participation, enlightened understanding, final control of the agenda by the *demos*, and inclusiveness (1985, 59-60). While Dahl does not say that the destruction of any one of these criteria could lead to tyranny, I believe it to be a reasonable inference to draw from Dahl's view of tyranny.

His criteria for a democratic process include both quantitative (political) and qualitative (social) elements (Roper 1989, 17). For example, equal votes represent the most quantitative criteria Dahl identifies as necessary for a democratic process. The remaining four criteria are more qualitative in their construction, although effective participation, final control of the agenda by the *demos*, and inclusiveness have quantitative components. Enlightened understanding appears to be the only criteria that are solely qualitative.

What this adds to the definition of tyranny is a number of new, or related qualitative factors, that if violated or destroyed, would lead to tyranny. I would argue that majority tyranny would be one possible outcome, but Dahl would likely disagree. Nevertheless, these additions do not change the substantive definition of tyranny as it was posed in chapter 4. Much of what Dahl had to say about Madison's definition was included in the reconstructed definition offered in chapter 2. Therefore, the definition as reconstructed from Madison, Dahl, Beahm, Fishkin, Roper, Tocqueville, and Calhoun remains: "Tyranny is every destruction of a right, as determined to be a right by the people, with no serious objections."

As before, this definition of tyranny encompasses all types of tyranny, including the definition of tyranny of the majority. Rights are at the center of Dahl's (or anyone's) understanding of the tyranny, because how rights are derived may well determine which ones will be protected, and how well they may be protected. In Dahl's case, how rights are perceived is tantamount to determining whether tyranny of the majority exists at all.

Dahl's Perception of Rights

Dahl believes that different perspectives on rights may influence how one views the relationship between democracy and rights. He identifies two distinct theoretical conceptions of rights. The first he refers to as the "theory of prior rights," and the second he identifies as rights necessary to the democratic process. The theory of prior rights is reflected in American constitutional thought, according to Dahl. These rights appear to him to be independent of democracy and the democratic process. They limit what is allowable within the democratic process by checking the process. Prior rights are considered to be not only anterior to the democratic process but superior to that process. Dahl notes that prior rights are sometimes viewed as being threatened by the democratic process, such as in cases of majority tyranny. However, he also believes that prior rights are often exercised at the expense of the democratic process (Dahl 1985, 24-25). He states:

> The liberty they make possible is potentially threatened by the democratic process. It follows that to preserve fundamental political rights and liberties a people must protect them from infringement by, among other things, the citizen body acting throughout the democratic process itself (Dahl 1985, 25).

The concern that Dahl has about the protection of prior rights is that the second theoretical concept of rights, the democratic process, may be compromised in the process of protecting them. For Dahl, the democratic process is of greater importance than prior rights, because it protects all of the fundamental rights necessary to self-government (Dahl 1985, 24-26). Dahl states:

> In this perspective, the right to self-government through the democratic process is itself one of the most fundamental rights that a person can possess. Indeed, if any rights can be said to be inalienable, surely this must be among them. Consequently, any infringement of the right to self-government must necessarily violate a fundamental, inalienable right. But if people are entitled to govern themselves, then citizens are also entitled to all the rights that are necessary in order for them to govern themselves—that is, all the rights that are essential to the democratic process. On this reasoning, a set of basic political rights can be derived from one of the most fundamental of all the rights to which human beings are entitled—the right of self-government (Dahl 1985, 25-26).

Dahl's interpretation of the democratic process would indicate that he supports the idea of social-compact/community-sanctioned rights, much as John Calhoun does. For Dahl the most important right is the right to self-government, and self-government empowers the citizens to chose which rights they will claim. Therefore, community-sanctioned rights logically fit his perception of rights much better than the prior-rights view.

Dahl holds that if the democratic process fails to protect fundamental rights, the result is the destruction of the democratic process. He considers this to be true even when a majority dominates a minority. He also finds it illogical for a people socialized in democracy to do anything but choose democracy, if what they truly value is the choice offered by the democratic process. Therefore, societies dedicated to democracy will not choose to destroy the democratic process by failure to protect fundamental rights, even those of the minority (Dahl 1985, 27-29; 1989, 170-73). Dahl does not think that the historical record of democratic regimes reveals much evidence of political rights being violated by the democratic process. He argues that

> the historical evidence to date seems to me to provide scant support for the view that the destruction of fundamental political rights by means of laws passed according to democratic procedures is a salient characteristic of democratic countries. As in comparison with all other regimes, historical and contemporary, modern democracies are, by comparison with their own earlier experience, unique in the scope of the political rights protected by law and the proportion of the adult population who may effectively exercise those rights (Dahl 1985, 24).

While few would argue that nondemocratic regimes have protected political rights as well as democratic regimes that have remained faithful to the democratic process, by Dahl's own admission, American history offers evidence of one of the most egregious violations of fundamental rights on record. He states, "Here a racial minority suffered a deprivation of fundamental political and human rights unequaled in any other democratic country both in the number of persons victimized and in the severity of the deprivations" (Dahl 1985, 23).

Dahl believes that the treatment of blacks was the exception to the historical rule in democratic regimes, because they were a "large minority" who gained "nominal citizenship only after a long period of slavery" and "were also racially distinct" (1985, 23). He further contends that, historically, "primary political rights" have been expanded, not contracted, in democratic regimes that follow the democratic process.

While Dahl may be correct about the expansion of primary political rights in America, the history of resistance to that expansion is also clear. I believe that many other minority groups in addition to blacks have had their fundamental political rights violated by way of the democratic process. The treatment of Native Americans, Hispanics, the Japanese during World War II, and the Mormons, to name a few, is evidence that there have been a number of exceptions to just treatment through the democratic process. The invoking of prior rights and constitutional checks has often prevented or corrected denials of fundamental political rights where the traditional democratic process (such as voting, and the passing of legislation) has faltered. I do not believe that these preventions and corrections are contrary to the democratic process.

I think it is apparent that Dahl's theory of prior rights is really just a renaming of natural rights. He does not clearly identify these rights (a criticism he correctly levels at Madison), but I assume them to be either the inalienable rights of life, liberty, and property (Locke 1947) (unless he is including Jefferson's interpretation from the Declaration of Independence, and finds "pursuit of happiness" to be more fulfilling), or the "key prerequisites of political democracy," which are "the right to vote, freedom of speech, freedom of assembly, and freedom of the press" (Dahl 1956, 59). Either way, he is unclear about which rights he is considering when he speaks of natural/prior rights.

What is clear is that Dahl does not support the notion of natural/prior rights (1956, 23, 45; 1985, 24-25). He states:

> Unless it is simply an elliptical mode of argument that might be cast in more precise language, the logic of natural rights seems to require a transcendental view in which the right is "natural" because God directly or indirectly wills it. God wills it as a right men ought to be (but not necessarily are) permitted by their fellows to exercise in society. It is easy to see that such an argument inevitably involves a variety of assumptions that at best are difficult and at worst impossible to prove to the satisfaction of anyone of positivist or skeptical predispositions (1956, 45).

These statements clearly put Dahl in the social-compact/community-sanction theoretical camp of rights. Although Dahl's interpretation of natural/prior rights is typical, I do not believe this is the only way to interpret natural rights. Natural rights can have a more secularized, or utilitarian, interpretation (Rossiter 1953, 366-67). For example, Tocqueville believes that citizens know how far they can be pushed because they have a sense of what their rights are (Tocqueville 1969, I: 237-38). I believe a natural right to be a right that is determined by the people to be natural to their sense of morality and justice. Of course this can be difficult to know for sure, but no one else can make this determination, and no other authority can better determine what rights people have than they themselves. As I contended in chapter 2, natural rights are what the people say they are.

One might argue that I am supporting the idea that rights are arrived at by way of the democratic process, similar to what Dahl would suggest. True. The difference is that I find Dahl to be too restrictive in how he delimits the democratic process. He does not believe that constitutional checks are necessary to the democratic process (1956, 21-22, 31; 1985, 24-31). Constitutional checks have become associated with natural/prior rights by way of American constitutional thought (Dahl 1985, 24), and this appears to be what disturbs Dahl. He does not endorse constitutional checks or natural/prior rights because they do not flow with the purity he would like to see in the democratic process.

Nevertheless, if constitutional checks were ratified as part of a democratic constitutional government, the use of these checks would be a part of the democratic process. Dahl asserts that the checks interfere with the democratic process and are thereby outside of it (Dahl 1956, 21-22). Nonetheless, if the citizens have approved the constitutional checks so that they might protect their political rights and liberties, I would find that to be consistent with the democratic process.

I contend that the constitutional checks and balances that serve to protect minorities from majority tyranny do not destroy the democratic process they are a part of it. Dahl is correct to hold that citizens have a right to the democratic process, but it is by that process that constitutional checks and balances came into existence (judicial review might be an exception). If the actual use of checks is destructive to the democratic process, then the citizens have chosen to destroy democracy and have selected some other form of government. Since Dahl does not believe a people desirous of the benefits of democracy can rightly choose any other form of government, he is in contradiction with himself over citizens' choosing to maintain constitutional checks that protect minorities, because they, in Dahl's eyes, would be destroying the democratic process (1985, 29). Surely, if the citizens had wanted to remove constitutional checks against majority tyranny, they would have used the democratic process to do so by now.

Dahl's Corrections to the Tyranny of the Majority

Dahl believes that "inherent social checks" (Dahl 1956, 22) will often prevent the majority from making decisions that would violate the rights of the minority. Dahl, then, is not opposed to restraining overbearing majorities if it needs to be done, but how it is done does matter. He states:

Every advocate of democracy of whom I am aware, and every friendly definition of it, includes the idea of restraints on majorities. But one central issue is
whether these restraints are, or should be, (1) primarily internalized restraints in
the individual behavior system, such as the conscience and other products of
social indoctrination, (2) primarily social checks and balances of several kinds,
or (3) primarily prescribed constitutional checks. Among political systems to
which the term "democracy" is commonly applied in the Western world, one
important difference is between those which rely primarily on the first two
checks, and those like the United States which also employ constitutional
checks (Dahl 1956, 36).

Madison strongly supported the implementation of constitutional checks
(Madison 1961, *Federalist 10* and *Federalist 51*). Dahl believes that internal
restraint and social checks and balances serve the purpose of controlling dominant majorities. Dahl goes so far as to argue that if social checks and balances
fail, constitutional checks will fail also. He surmises that

the Madisonian argument exaggerates the importance, in preventing tyranny, of
specified checks to governmental officials by other specified governmental officials; it underestimates the importance of the inherent social checks and balances existing in every pluralistic society. Without these social checks and balances, it is doubtful that the intragovernmental checks on officials would in fact
operate to prevent tyranny; with them, it is doubtful that all of the intragovernmental checks of the Madisonian system as it operates in the United States are
necessary to prevent tyranny (Dahl 1956, 22).

Dahl's position is at least partially accurate. No doubt inherent social checks
and balances play a major role in preventing the most outlandish spectacles of
majority tyranny. Internalized restraints such as one's conscience most assuredly
act to limit irresponsible behavior. It, in all probability, would be hard to over-
emphasize the importance of these deterrents to majority domination at the expense of minority rights. Nonetheless, the constitutional checks on tyrannical
majorities cannot be underestimated in any consideration of restraints on the
public, or on public officials.

What Dahl does not account for are the innumerable times that majoritarian
tyranny has been stifled by these constitutional checks. Presidential vetoes, the
Senate voting down a bill approved by the House of Representatives, and judicial review has frequently acted to squelch an insistent majority that would have
done harm to minority concerns. All too often even these checks have been inadequate to stop the majority from tyrannizing the minority. To diminish protection of the minority by relying on the inherent self-controlling nature of individuals, and the societal pressure to behave fairly, would be to expect too much
of these personal and social phenomena.

I believe that Dahl underestimates the ability of constitutional checks to
limit the challenges to minority rights. The sheer fact that these checks exist may

act as a deterrent to majority tyranny. In the case where the checks are actually needed, their utilization may well prevent a further breakdown in minority protection. If the political culture does break down, constitutional checks will probably not prevent the final collapse, but at that point there would probably be a lot more wrong with the democratic process than just the constitutional checks.

Dahl wants to support equality by way of procedural democracy. He believes that any negative, other than internal and societal restraints, will reduce equality (1956, 31-33, 63-85; 1996, 639-48). The problem with this contention is that, historically, procedural democracy has not produced equality, particularly in the area of racial equality. This seems to be ignored by Dahl in his book *Who Governs?*, even when his own research reveals the same thing (1961). The purity of procedural democracy may suffer at times from the use of constitutional checks, but rarely is a determined majority deterred from attaining its desired outcome. If a majority must violate minority rights to achieve its objectives, then a part of the political process has temporarily broken down, and a restoration of the process may most fairly be achieved by the very constitutional checks he opposes.

Lani Guinier believes the system has been broken for some time. She finds that blacks are consistently underrepresented in the political system as it is. The following discussion examines her views on the tyranny of the majority and looks toward potential solutions to the problem.

Guinier's Tyranny of the Majority

The essence of Lani Guinier's conceptualization of the tyranny of the majority is that "winner-take-all" (1994, 55, 79, 82), "single-member districts" (82-86), deny blacks "authentic representation" (55-58). She believes that when majority rule is exercised under winner-take-all rules, confidence in the fairness of the system is undermined for minorities because they rarely end up represented in a meaningful way (79). She does not believe that single-member districts have been the panacea to black representation that they had once been thought, particularly at the municipal and county government level (82-83). If blacks are not represented through community-based, community-accountable leadership, their representation, for Guinier, is not authentic. By contrast, some define authenticity as simple physiological and cultural representation. This view of authenticity relies on black representatives being "elected by blacks" and being "descriptively similar to their constituents. In other words, they are politically, psychologically, and culturally black" (1994, 56). When defined simply in terms of shared descriptive features or common cultural experience, authenticity for Guinier "is a limited empowerment tool" (58). Given Guinier's more robust view of the term, "authentic" and "authentic representation" will be used here to characterize community-based, community-accountable representation. When Guinier adopts as her own the term authentic, she intends to convey the notion of dynamic and engaged indigenous leadership and not simply to refer to elected officials who happen to share some attributes in common with their constituents (44-46).[1]

It is Guinier's opinion that a society as racially divided as ours must have a system of representation that provides for diverse groups, or it loses legitimacy. Winner-take-all districting does not fulfill this need, because the dominant group in each district ends up with all of the power. She contends that "the one-person, one-vote doctrine is consistent with both group and individual conceptions of voting," but not in winner-take-all districting, where votes are not equal. When one group consistently wins and others consistently lose, a number of votes are wasted, thereby destroying the concept of the equal vote (1994, 121-23).

Guinier insists that the "inherent legitimacy of winner-take-all majority rule" should be questioned, instead of focusing on whether "minority rights trump majoritarian democracy." She claims that "disproportionate majority power is, in itself, so wrong that it delegitimizes majority rule." It is wrong because it does not take into account the importance or intensity of minority interests and therefore doesn't encourage minority groups to support outcomes or believe that they will be "public-regarding or legitimate" (Guinier 1994, 102-3). Furthermore, Guinier states:

> I would argue that majority rule is unfair in situations where the majority is racially prejudiced against the minority to such a degree that the majority consistently excludes the minority, or refuses to inform itself about the relative merit of the minority's preferences. This is because the claim that majority rule is legitimate rests on the two main assumptions that do not hold where racial prejudice pervades the majority: (1) that majorities are fluid rather than fixed; and (2) that minorities will be able to become part of the governing coalition in the future (Guinier 1994, 103).

Since whites make up the majority, at least in the South, and this is unlikely to change for some time, it is clear that the majority is fixed. Due to a number of factors, minorities have not been included in the governing coalition. It is not likely, given the permanent division that the white majority perpetuates, that minority interests will be seriously taken into consideration when governmental decisions are made. In all likelihood minority interests will be marginalized. Majority rule is transformed into majority tyranny because racism keeps minorities from being part of the ruling majority (Guinier 1994, 103).

Guinier argues that blacks continue to be discouraged from participating fully in the democratic process because winner-take-all districts discourage participation and lead to what she calls "partial democracy. "Partial democracy" is characterized by Guinier as democracy that doesn't promote full participation or inclusion in the democratic process. She contends that when less than a majority

---

[1] THE TYRANNY OF THE MAJORITY: Fundamental Fairness in Representative Democracy by Lani Guinier. New York: The Free Press: an imprint of Simon & Schuster Adult Publishing Group, 1994.

of the eligible electorate turns out to vote, government "of," "by," and "for" the people is failing. Those who did not vote for the governing party, or "losers," are particularly dissatisfied with "the way democracy works" (Guinier 1998, 251-53).

However, Guinier submits that there is much more to full participation than just voting. She states "that voting is a rather trivial measure of democracy." To emphasize voter turnout would be to minimize the need to participate in the process every day of the year. Getting people involved in the political process by encouraging them to join "political organizations, parties, and citizens' groups is essential to a more participatory democracy " (1998, 251-53).

So, according to Guinier, winner-take-all elections discourage participation at a number of different levels. They not only discourage voters who consistently lose at the polls, but they also discourage them from participating in the groups that might promote political activity that would be helpful to their cause. Guinier complains that the "effect of our partial democracy is particularly egregious on poor people" (1998, 253). She states that "in 1990, 13.8 percent of American voters came from families with incomes under $15,000; in 1992, those low-income voters declined to 11.0 percent of voters; in 1994, they were just 7.7 percent" (1998, 253).

There are a number of reasons why low-income voters do not turn out at election time. One of those reasons, according to Guinier, is that winner-take-all elections produce elected officials who do not address the issues of the poor. Since their interests are not being addressed, the indigents become increasingly disenchanted with the political process. Low-income voters are further discouraged from participating in the process because the candidates who do get elected do not see the poor as a voting bloc that can help them get reelected. Partial democracy creates a vicious cycle that perpetuates the downward cycle of participation (1998, 251-53).

Guinier also asserts that the winner-take-all system preserves the two major parties at the expense of alternative parties that would represent a greater variety of views. She believes that being limited to two parties "encourages centrism but not necessarily consensus," because candidates have "to move to the middle where most of the votes are." This limits the effectiveness of dissent, because dissenters are increasingly pushed outside the realm of influence. Once in office the incumbent knows which constituency aided in his/her election and can effectively ignore those that did not assist that endeavor (1998, 254).

Moreover, Guinier maintains that winner-take-all geographic districting results in representatives selecting voters, rather than voters selecting representatives. The power of incumbency allows representatives to draw election district lines around their supporters, thereby almost ensuring victory in their next election. This promotes continued monopolization of power by groups that dominate in particular districts (1998, 255). While this has allowed blacks the opportunity to win some districts that they otherwise would not have, Guinier does not support this type of districting. She states:

The essential unfairness of districting is a result, therefore, of two assumptions: (1) that a majority of voters within a given geographic community can be configured to constitute a "group"; and (2) that incumbent politicians, federal courts, or some other independent set of actors can fairly determine which group to advantage by giving it all the power within the district. When either of these assumptions is not accurate, as is most often the case, the districting is necessarily unfair (1994, 121).

Guinier insists "that on some level all districting is gerrymandering." This is done not only to increase the power of some groups in districts, but also to diminish the "overall influence" of minorities throughout a number of districts by packing them into a few. She alleges that even race-conscious districting isolates blacks into certain districts, and leaves other white districts isolated from black voter influence. Guinier fears that race-conscious districting will also create a situation where there will be more blacks serving as representatives to districts in the legislature, but they will be as disarmed and racially isolated there as the blacks living in districts where their voices are not heard (1994, 135).

Guinier, and others, find that the racial districting that was once thought to be a key to electing blacks turned out not to be a guarantee that blacks would be well represented. Often when blacks were elected to public office they were still outvoted by the white majority. Additionally, blacks that were elected from single-member districts became so enmeshed in maintaining their incumbency, that they began to confuse being in office with actually having influence. Guinier states that "the 'black faces in high places' litigation strategy failed to realize that the color of the advocate alone does not determine political efficacy. We confused presence with power in ways that often led to the demobilization of our real sources of strength and voice—an organized constituency that backed up our demands and allowed our elected officials to speak and be heard" (1998, 257).

Guinier had discovered that the "winner-gets-all, loser-gets-none system" (1998, 254) resulted "in the minority—whether racial, political, cultural, or occupational"—being disadvantaged. If one has "a different perspective or political identity," regardless of the shape of the district, minority status ensures that you "have virtually no chance of being represented by someone" whom you "actually voted for" (1998, 257). For Guinier, racism or other prejudices that exclude minority points of view from the political process cause majority tyranny. Winner-take-all majoritarian systems, such as single-member districting, are the methods by which majoritarian tyranny is carried out (1994, 103).

Guinier's Addition to the Definition of Tyranny

Guinier does not specifically define tyranny, or the tyranny of the majority. She seemingly endorses Madison's definition of tyranny, and she even refers to "a majority that rules but does not dominate" as a "Madisonian Majority" (1994, 3-4). Beyond supporting Madison's ideas on what tyranny is, Guinier offers two contributions of her own. She identifies winner-take-all districting (1994, 55, 79, 82-86, 121) and the lack of authentic representation for blacks (1994, 55-58) as two forms of majority tyranny.

For Guinier, winner-take-all districting leads to a lack of authentic representation for blacks and other groups (1994, 55-58, 79). Winner-take-all districting does not promote the election of representatives from diverse points of view, because districts are gerrymandered to provide an advantage to the white majority (1994, 17, 102-3, 121-23, 135). This discourages minorities from participating at all levels and leads to fewer blacks and other minorities from being elected to public office (1998, 251-53). Therefore, blacks and other minorities do not receive representation that truly reflects their cultural dispositions (1994, 55-58).

Winner-take-all districting adds another quantitative (political) element to the definition of tyranny. It is quantitative because it is about how votes determine winners within a particular system. The lack of authentic representation adds another qualitative (social) element to the definition of tyranny. It is qualitative because it is about the social phenomena of blacks not being culturally represented in the system, and being discouraged from participating in the system. A lack of authentic representation might be interpreted as a quantitative element, because it is also about a lack of black representatives, but the social aspect seems to me to be the more pertinent of the two.

Though both of these new elements add dimensions to the definition of tyranny, they do not substantively change the definition. The definition remains the same because winner-take-all districts that lead to a lack of authentic representation would be the destruction of a right, as Guinier understands it. Therefore, the reconstructed definition of tyranny derived from Madison, Dahl, Beahm, Fishkin, Roper, Tocqueville, Calhoun, and Guinier continues to be, "Tyranny is every destruction of a right, as determined to be a right by the people, with no serious objections."

As with all previous definitions of tyranny, this definition includes all types of tyranny, including the definition of the tyranny of the majority. Guinier finds that majoritarian tyranny interferes with one's right to have one's vote count, which is inextricably tied up with one's right to be truly represented.

Guinier's Perception of Rights

Guinier's discussion of rights, as it relates to the tyranny of the majority, is to the point and can be summarized briefly. She believes that all people have a right to vote and to expect their vote to have some influence on who represents them (1994, 35-36, 123, 126, 55-58, 102-3). An important part of anyone's vote being represented in a meaningful way depends upon whether the group he or she is a part of is also represented. Beyond the individual and his associated group being represented, Guinier considers it essential that representation extend into the legislature. She appears to base her understanding of rights on the natural rights doctrine, but I can find no other indication of her theoretical view of rights except for the use of the word "nature" in the first sentence of the following quote. This quote nicely summarizes Guinier's opinion on what rights are most important. She insists that

> first, the fundamental nature of the right to vote stems from its role in preserving all other rights. Other rights, even the most basic, are illusory if the right to vote is undermined. The franchise gives status to the individual voter but derives its vitality from its exercise by a "politically cohesive" group of citizens who elect representatives to promote consideration of group interests in public policy. A voice in the process of self-government is heard only through the medium of elected representatives; the opportunity to vote is the vital means of affecting representation. Unlike other government benefits, the right to vote is therefore a meaningful entitlement. For the minority, the meaningful right to vote must include the correlative opportunity to elect a representative of that group's choice. . . . Second, equal status as participants within the political sphere is possible only if members of the group are allowed to participate at all stages of the process. . . . A meaningful right to vote contemplates minority participation in post-election legislative policymaking as well as pre-election coalition building and deliberation (1994, 35-36).

Guinier knows that if "whites refuse to work with or vote for a black candidate," her ideal has little hope of succeeding. Her plan for including blacks and other minorities in the electoral and legislative process is to have an alternative voting system implemented. This change would mean a drastic shift in the method by which voters select their candidates, but it would also alter the way in which voters would be represented. It is a bold plan, and one I think worthy of serious consideration.

Guinier's Corrections to the Tyranny of the Majority

In her two books, *The Tyranny of the Majority* and *Lift Every Voice*, Guinier offers several corrections to majoritarian tyranny. In *The Tyranny of the Majority*, Guinier suggests that "interest representation" (1994, 117-18), brought about by "cumulative voting" (1994, 14-16, 94-95, 119, 123, 137), would provide minorities (particularly blacks) a better and fairer opportunity to have their votes count and be adequately represented. In *Lift Every Voice*, Guinier suggests several ways in which to achieve interest representation through proportional representation. The proportional representation models that she identifies are the party listing system, preference voting, and her favorite, cumulative voting (1998, 258).

The party listing system that Guinier identifies was chosen in South Africa as part of their "negotiated transition to democracy," after rejecting winner-take-all elections that would have left the white minority poorly represented (1998, 258). In this system

> South Africa used proportional representation to assure seats in the national assembly for political parties in proportion to the percentage of votes cast for that party. The National Party (white Afrikaners) received 20.39 percent of the votes cast and got 20.5 percent of the seats in the national assembly. The African National Congress (Nelson Mandela's party) received 62.65 percent of the votes and 63.0 percent of the seats. The Inkatha Freedom Party (Chief Buthelezi) polled 10.54 percent of the votes and got 10.75 percent of the seats. A total of seven parties qualified for representation in the national assembly. In addition, the three parties with more than 5 percent of the national assembly seats were each awarded a number of cabinet portfolios. . . . Voters vote for a political party. The party fields a list of potential candidates. Not all of the party's candidates will win, unless the party gets 100 percent of the total number of votes cast. The candidates on the party list are only elected in direct proportion to the number of votes cast for the party they represent (Guinier 1998, 258).

I think that Guinier's implicit message in using this particular example speaks volumes about the inherent racism in America, where changing the voting system to provide blacks, or any other minority, a greater opportunity to be represented is unlikely.

According to Guinier, in the proportional representation system of preference voting, voters list their candidates as their first, second, or third order of preference (1998, 258). She explains, "The first choice ballots are counted first. When a candidate is elected by a sufficient number of those who picked him or her as first choice, the remaining ballots are counted toward their second or third choice, thus minimizing potentially wasted votes" (1998, 258).

Guinier claims that this system is still used in Cambridge, Massachusetts, and was previously used to elect New York City Council members. The result of applying this system in New York City was an increase in voter turnout and the number of candidates for office. What killed preference voting in New York City was the Democratic Party machine and fear of communism. Some Democrats felt threatened by the increased number of third-party candidates, but it was the specter of communism that suggested that proportional representation was "un-American," "undemocratic, and a threat to the two-party system" (Guinier 1998, 258, 264-65).

The final proportional representation system that Guinier proposes is cumulative voting. She explains that

> under cumulative voting, voters get the same number of votes as there are seats or options to vote for, and they can then distribute their votes in any combination to reflect their preferences. Like-minded voters can vote as a solid bloc or, instead, form strategic, cross-racial coalitions to gain mutual benefits. This system is emphatically not racially based; it allows voters to organize themselves on whatever basis they wish (1994, 14-15).

The principle of one person, one vote is upheld with cumulative voting because each voter has the same number of total votes (1994, 15). Guinier characterizes cumulative voting as a "semiproportionate" system; votes do not translate as directly into seats in the same way that proportionate election systems do. In a proportionate election system the number of seats won is equal to the percent of the vote won by that group. In the semiproportionate election system even a "politically cohesive group of voters is not guaranteed representation." Because votes can be spread in an array of options, victory is never certain (1998, 260).

Guinier holds that cumulative voting "could increase voter choice, by giving voters more votes to cast in support of their preferred candidates." She believes that this increased choice would act as an incentive "for local, grass-roots organizations to educate voters and sustain voter mobilization." In Guinier's view, "diverse minorities" would be strengthened by their options, "without dividing the electorate along racial lines or along the lines of winners and losers." With all of the improvements that cumulative voting may bring, Guinier states,

> there is a final benefit from cumulative voting. It eliminates gerrymandering. By denying protected incumbents safe seats in gerrymandered districts, cumulative voting might encourage more voter participation. With greater interest-based electoral competition, cumulative voting could promote the political turnover sought by advocates of term limits. In this way, cumulative voting serves many of the same ends as periodic elections or rotation in office, a solution that Madison and others advocated as a means of protecting against permanent majority factions (1994, 17).

In conjunction with applying cumulative voting to the electoral system generally, Guinier suggests that it could also be applied to the internal legislative voting process. What she proposes is for legislatures to vote on multiple bills that "would be aggregated or linked," instead of "voting up or down on individual proposals." By using "weighted and split issue voting," Guinier believes that black representatives (I believe that she would include anyone with a minority point of view) could better participate in the process by "plumping," or "trading votes," in order to reflect constituency preferences or indifference. Requiring supermajority votes "on issues of importance to the majority" or imposing " a minority veto on critical minority issues" would generally serve the same purpose as cumulative voting (198, 107-8).

Guinier understands that proportional representation voting systems of all types have been criticized for allowing the "minor political parties" to hold the "larger political parties hostage to their demands." She rejects this contention, explaining that it isn't proportional representation that causes this problem but the low threshold for inclusion of minor parties. She recommends that the threshold for including minority parties in legislature be set at 5 percent, as is now done in Germany, rather than the one percent that the Israelis have set for inclusion of minor parties in the Knesset (1998, 268-69).

Guinier states that she particularly likes "the mixed system now used in Germany" (1998, 269). I concur. What I don't understand is why she endorses the semiproportional representation system of cumulative voting, as opposed to a proportional representation system that is like Germany's mixed system, South Africa's party listing system, or a preference voting system where voters can rank candidates at their discretion (1998, 258). In her effort to "reenergize democracy," Guinier thinks that cumulative voting was a compromise between proportional systems like South Africa's and the winner-take-all system in the United States (1998, 260). She does not explain why she thinks she has to compromise between these two, rather than push for a proportional voting system that would be, in my estimation, simpler and more likely to represent minority interests.

What Dahl and Guinier Might Say to Each Other

Dahl does not have much to say about proportional representation (PR for short) except to state that

> the fact is that outside the English-speaking countries proportional representation is the norm. PR and multiparty systems do tend to go together. Typically in PR countries electorates are fragmented. A single party rarely wins a majority of seats, much less a majority of electoral votes. Coalition cabinets are the rule. And stable coalitions typically require consensus building (1989, 159-60).

From this it is difficult to know what Dahl would have thought about semiproportional cumulative voting systems. He clearly supports the democratic process (1985, 23-29; 1989, 170-73), but whether he would approve of Guinier's proposals for changing it is not apparent.

What we can be certain about is that Dahl would not have supported Guinier's arguments that majoritarian tyranny exists, and that there is a need to eliminate it (Dahl 1956, 4-33; 1985, 13-31; 1989, 171-73; Guinier 1994, 1-20). He would have also found the need for external constitutional checks against democratic procedure to be without warrant (Dahl 1956, 22, 36; Guinier 1994, 108). Dahl would generally find Guinier's efforts to include minorities further in the democratic process redundant, because he believes that minorities already rule (Dahl 1956, 133; Guinier 1994, 79, 103, 117-18).

Dahl would want Guinier to know that the American system of government is not a static one. He believes that it has survived because it has evolved through many changes. For the most part, Dahl is convinced that the American political system works. Although he would not necessarily suggest it for export to other countries, he is persuaded that it has served us well (1956, 150-51). He concludes that "so long as the social prerequisites of democracy are substantially intact in this country, it appears to be a relatively efficient system for reinforcing agreement, encouraging moderation, and maintaining social peace in a restless and immoderate people operating a gigantic, powerful, diversified, and incredibly complex society" (1956, 151).

I believe that Guinier would respond by telling Dahl that she supports the democratic process also, but that the process in place in America has acted to the disadvantage of blacks and other minorities. The system works for the white majority, but not for minorities, who are unable to be authentically and adequately represented (1994, 55-58). She would say that the tyranny of majority exists because the majority is fixed rather than fluid, and minorities will not "be able to become part of the governing coalition in the future" without major changes in how we pick our representatives at all levels (1994, 102-3).

It is likely that Guinier would find less need for external constitutional checks if the democratic procedures were more interest representative (1994, 94-102).She would contend that the elimination of the winner-take-all, single-member districting system (1994, 55, 79, 82-86), along with the development of a semiproportionate cumulative voting system, would go a long way toward reducing the need for external checks and balances (1994, 14-16, 94-95, 119, 123, 137). She would insist that the "solution to the tyranny of The Majority" is "more democracy, not less" (1994, 20). Undoubtedly, Guinier would maintain that a move toward a more proportionate system of voting would be a move toward more democracy and greater participation of all types by a larger number of citizens. Dahl would support the idea of a more participatory democracy, but whether he would accept Guinier's procedural changes is in doubt.

Dahl and Guinier demonstrate some of the differences that still exist over the issue of majority tyranny. They both share some similarities with John Calhoun. How those distinctions and similarities blend to create the mixture of theories on the subject of the tyranny of the majority is the subject of the final chapter.

References

Dahl, Robert A. 1956. *A Preface to Democratic Theory*. Chicago: University of Chicago Press.

———. 1961. *Who Governs? Democracy and Power in an American City*. New Haven, Conn.: Yale University Press.

———. 1985. *A Preface to Economic Democracy*. Berkeley: University of California Press.

———. 1989. *Democracy and Its Critics*. New Haven, Conn.: Yale University Press.

———. 1996. "Equality versus Inequality." *Political Science & Politics:* December 1996. Vol. 29. No. 4: 639-48.

Fishkin, James S. 1979. *Tyranny and Legitimacy: A Critique of Political Theories*. Baltimore: Johns Hopkins University Press.

Guinier, Lani. 1994. *The Tyranny of the Majority: Fundamental Fairness in Representative Democracy*. Foreword by Stephen L. Carter. New York: Free Press.

————. 1998. *Lift Every Voice: Turning a Civil Rights Setback into a New Vision of Social Justice*. New York: Simon and Schuster.

Locke, John. 1947. *Two Treatises of Government*. With a supplement *Patriarcha* by Robert Filmer. Ed. with an introduction by Thomas I. Cook. New York: Hafner.

Madison, James. With Alexander Hamilton and John Jay. 1961. *The Federalist Papers*. Introduction by Clinton Rossiter. New York: New American Library.

Piven, Frances Fox, and Richard A. Cloward. 1988. *Why Americans Don't Vote*. New York: Pantheon.

Peterson, Svend. 1963. *A Statistical History of American Presidential Elections*. New York: Frederic Ungar.

Roper, Jon. 1989. *Democracy and Its Critics: Anglo-American Democratic Thought in the Nineteenth Century*. London: Unwin Hyman.

Rossiter, Clinton. 1953. *Seedtime of the Republic: The Origin of the American Tradition of Political Liberty*. New York: Harcourt, Brace.

Safford, John L. 1995. "John C. Calhoun, Lani Guinier, and Minority Rights." *Political Science & Politics*: June 1995. Vol. 26. No. 2: 211-16.

Scammon, Richard. 1991. *America Votes 19*. Washington D.C.: Congressional Quarterly.

Talmon, J. L. 1970. *The Origins of Totalitarian Democracy*. New York: Norton.

Tocqueville, Alexis de. 1969. *Democracy in America*. Trans. George Lawrence. Ed. J. P. Mayer. New York: Harper and Row.

Chapter 6

A Synthesis of Perspectives on the American Dilemma

In this chapter I will synthesize the perspectives of Madison, Tocqueville, Calhoun, Dahl, and Guinier on the subject of the tyranny of the majority. This synthesis will include the same four points of clarification and analysis that have been applied to each of the authors in the preceding chapters. I will begin with a synthesis of the alternative conceptions of the tyranny of the majority, in order to bring some cohesiveness to the central issue of this study. By examining the alternative conceptions of the tyranny of the majority I have attempted to clarify the authors' various perceptions of the subject. In this section I will bring all of those perceptions together with the intent of suggesting a more meaningful construction of the idea of the tyranny of the majority.

The second point to be synthesized will be the authors' definitions of tyranny. To define the tyranny of the majority I felt it was first necessary to define tyranny by adding each author's perspective. What I have discovered from attempting to define tyranny this way is that the definition of the tyranny of the majority is subsumed within the definition of tyranny. Therefore, through the process of reconstructing the definition of tyranny I have synthesized the definition of both tyranny and the tyranny of the majority. Nevertheless, I will briefly present a review of the definitions of tyranny to establish my interpretation of its meaning, consistent with the synthesis of the alternative conceptions of the tyranny of the majority.

Thirdly, a synthesis of the authors' perceptions of rights will be undertaken to demonstrate how they have influenced thinking about the tyranny of the majority. All theories of the tyranny of the majority are based on how a particular theorist views rights. I will provide a brief review of each author's view of rights, and then suggest which approach is the most conducive to a theory of the tyranny of the majority. Perceptions of rights often influence what corrections are offered to alleviate majoritarian tyranny.

Fourthly, the alternative corrections to the tyranny of the majority will be synthesized in an effort to suggest further steps that might be taken to remedy the problem. Each author has suggested ways in which tyrannical majorities might be dealt with, but they vary considerably, and some appear more likely to be effective than others. I will conclude this section with my ideas on how to correct for the tyranny of the majority.

A Synthesis of the Tyranny of the Majority

Majority tyranny begins with the people, but in a representative democracy, majority tyranny makes its way into the government—mostly into the legislature (Madison 1961, 51:322; Tocqueville 1969, 155; Calhoun 3-25; Guinier 1994, 55, 79, 82-86). This progressive expansion from the people to the institutions of government follows a general pattern. Once this pattern is discerned the alternative conceptions can be better understood. A unified general theory of the tyanny of the majority cannot be claimed here, because this study is limited to some, but not all, of the most important contributors on the issue. Also, I have focused on the American dilemma to avoid the confusion of applying the concepts to multiple societies and political systems.

Among all the different ways to evaluate the concepts of the tyranny of the majority, Jon Roper has found one of the most efficient for categorizing them. He has identified the political aspects of majority tyranny as "quantitative," and the social aspects as "qualitative." While the quantitative aspects of majority tyranny have usually been obvious (majorities dominating at the polls, or in the legislature), qualitative aspects have not been as readily apparent (such as factions, equality, public opinion, and the press). As Roper states, "The majority not only won votes and determined policies, it also influenced attitudes" (1989, 17).

Understanding the social aspects of majority tyranny is especially important to comprehending Madison's and Tocqueville's conceptualizations. Madison believes the cause of majority tyranny to be factions. He thinks that an overbearing majority faction pursuing its interest with a vengeance is what we should fear. Importantly, he also believes that factions can stifle majoritarian tyranny by canceling each other out (1961, 10:77-84).

Tocqueville finds the threat of tyrannical majorities to emanate from citizens' lust for equality, which leads them to sameness in their opinions. He is concerned that the striving to be equal causes people to want to be too much alike, and that by doing so they become intolerant of differences (Tocqueville 1969, 1:57, 2:254-56, 2:435-36).He also thinks that associations, much like factions for Madison, can also deter majoritarian oppression (1969, 1:189-95).

Both Calhoun and Guinier believe that the political process suffers from inadequacies that lead to tyrannical majorities dominating policy making, but they appreciate the effects that social causes have on majoritarian tyranny. Calhoun identifies self-interestedness as the key ingredient that motivates people's behavior. Since humans are social beings, they have tendencies to congregate in groups that share interests. The larger of these groups can come to dominate the others, thereby tyrannizing the minority (Calhoun 1953, 3-14).

Calhoun holds that the use of political parties is the cause of majoritarian tyranny (Spain 1951, 108-17). He thinks that numerical majorities exercising their authority through suffrage is what brings the tyranny about (1953, 19-25). Calhoun suggests that every individual interest seek a mode of expression and favor. Political parties provide the avenue for those expressions. The danger is that too often parties become an end unto themselves, and they don't serve the purposes of the broader society. The press is similar to suffrage in that it is an expression of public opinion. Calhoun argues that the press stirs up partisan conflict by igniting public opinion, which leads to majoritarian tyranny by the party that can win the next election by numerical majority (Calhoun 1953, 56-58; Spain 1951, 108-17). The party in power uses its authority to offer patronage to those who have helped their cause (Spain 1951, 111), and it punishes its enemies by taxing them unequally (Calhoun 1953, 16-19).

Guinier asserts that minority interests are not well served by the winner-take-all system of representation used in America (1994, 55, 79, 82). In fact, she believes that winner-take-all, single-member districts to be the cause of majoritarian tyranny (1994, 55, 79, 82-86). Much like Calhoun, she finds suffrage to be the method that brings majoritarian tyranny about. She makes the case that interest representation and cumulative voting would help blacks achieve authentic representation (1994, 117-18, 14-16, 119, 123, 137, 55-58).

In Guinier's opinion, majority interests often marginalize blacks and other minority groups, keeping them from being full participants in the social, as well as political, process of governing (1998, 251-53). Racism keeps minorities from having their interests accounted for in the political process, and leads to majoritarian tyranny (1994, 103). Guinier thinks that if the interests of minority groups are not eventually appreciated, these groups will begin to look for alternative solutions outside of the political system (1994, 51).

Even Dahl acknowledges that social influences play the predominant role in how effectively the political process works. He argues that social training in the norms of society and social checks against majority tyranny are more influential in controlling tyrannical majorities than external constitutional checks (1956, 36, 78, 80-81). Dahl asserts that "social prerequisites," necessary to a democratic society functioning well, "may be far more important in strengthening democracy than any particular constitutional design" (1956, 83).

I believe Dahl to be wrong about external constitutional checks under the present system of government in America, but I think he is correct about the importance of social influences on how the government operates. Social influences act as the impetus for many political actions, including those affecting the tyranny of the majority. These social or qualitative influences are often the bed-rock causes of majority tyranny, but it is easy to look past them to the more evident political causes. Nevertheless, there are two qualitative influences that I believe have more effect on theories of the tyranny of the majority than any others—individual and group interests.

The common thread that runs through all of the conceptualizations of the tyranny of the majority is that of individual interests being expressed through groups. Madison's factions are really just groups of individuals with particular interests, that are "adverse to the rights of other citizens, or to the permanent and aggregate interests of the community" (Madison 1961, *Federalist 10:*78). Tocqueville fears that individuals are more at risk of majority tyranny when they become "isolated and weak." It is the pursuit of individual interests that causes them to lose appreciation for the "common good." He believes that associations help to alleviate this problem (Lamberti 1989, 82; Tocqueville 1969, 1:189-95, 2:513-16). Calhoun perceives that it is the use of political parties by the majority to achieve individual interests that causes majority tyranny (Calhoun 1953, 3-25; Spain 1951, 108-17). Guinier's view of interest representation is based on the idea that individual minorities are not adequately represented unless their particular groups are represented (1994, 94-99).

Hence, I believe that the causes of majoritarian tyranny lead back to individual interests that are expressed through organized groups. Since individuals alone cannot influence the system, they must join in concert with other individuals through groups. These groups may be civic or political (Tocqueville 1969, 513-17), but at some point they must become political to influence the political system. These groups may eventually develop into political parties, or greatly affect the priorities of parties that already exist.

Once individuals have organized themselves into groups powerful enough to act, they must have a political process that is amenable to making their inputs felt. If the group is powerful enough, and the democratic process allows or encourages it in some way, that group may develop into a tyrannical majority. Therefore, it is my contention that individual interests acting in concert through groups or parties bring about majoritarian tyranny, in a democratic system that lends itself to the development of tyrannical majorities. I would argue that the American democratic republic is such a political system.

The democratic political process in America encourages the formation of tyrannical majorities by its two-party system, its winner-take-all districting, and through the voting system. Beyond individual and group interests being the primary cause of majority tyranny, the two-party system limits the interest of a number of potential voters. The limitation of the two major-party candidates in most congressional races narrows the choices that many voters might make if a broader variety of candidates were available. As Guinier has suggested, the two-party system is also a function of the winner-take-all districting (1994, 254; 1998, 258, 265-66). She states that

districting tends to promote a two-party system by "avoiding a splintering mul-
tiparty development." Although such a system, in which third parties are all but
doomed to perpetual defeat, is perceived as more stable than a coalition government, it tends to promote stability at the cost of representing minority interests. In a two-party system, interests are only protected to the extent they garner
majority support or merit judicial protection by virtue of the majority's violation of the minority's right to equal protection. Districting, therefore, does
nothing to promote active consideration of minority interests; instead, it forces
minority voter and representatives to compromise and adjust their interests to
the informal constructs provided by one of the two major parties, thereby reducing the representation of minority interests. In this way, districting can reduce the interest representation of minorities to arbitrary, fixed choices. In fact,
it may be that the two-party structure associated with the districting system has
disconnected voters from the process of self-government (1994, 85-85).

Winner-take-all districting promotes wasted votes by minority interests,
who come out on the losing side most of the time (Guinier 1994, 121-23). When
the candidates of minorities continually lose, it discourages full participation in
the political process. The decrease in the number of voters in presidential and
congressional elections is indicative of the "partial democracy" that has evolved
from this lack of participation (Guinier 1998, 251-53). Winner-take-all districting promotes majoritarian tyranny because it limits minority input into the political system.

The voting system in America also encourages majoritarian tyranny in at
least three ways. First, voting is only allowed on a single day (usually Tuesday)
for any one election. This limits the number of people who can make it to the
polls due to work schedules, illness, transportation problems, and a host of other
reasons. Second, most legislative seats in the country are set up as single-
member districts, where those who lose in the election receive no representation,
creating more losers than winners, if those who don't vote are counted. Third,
the winner-take-all system of districting is also a system of voting which requires voters to pick one of usually two candidates. It also promotes more losers
than winners, leaving many votes wasted on candidates who won't serve any
representational function.

Madison, Tocqueville, Calhoun, and Guinier address the faults in the democratic process that encourage majority tyranny. Madison was so busy constructing the system that he didn't have time, or the benefit of hindsight, to do a full
analysis. Nevertheless, he understood that factions would cause trouble, and that
checks and balances would need to be available to thwart their threat to minority
interests. Madison increased our understanding of both political and social
causes of majoritarian tyranny, but he did not predict that winner-take-all districts would facilitate majority tyranny in the way that it has.

Tocqueville does more to increase awareness of the social causes of majority tyranny than any of the other theorists. His focus on equality as a social cause
leading to majority tyranny is both stunning and insightful (1969, 1:57, 1:254-
56, 2:435-36). His book *Democracy in America* stands as one of the premier

analyses of the social and political aspects of America ever achieved. Nonetheless, he does make one error that I believe is worth pointing out regarding associations. Tocqueville sees only the positive side of associations, not the negative. He believes that associations can help save us from tyrannical majorities. What he fails to see is that they may also lead to tyrannical majorities (Tocqueville 1969, 1:189-95).

Calhoun may have the most balanced approach to understanding the political and social causes of majoritarian tyranny of any of the theorists. His grasp of the social process of majority tyranny, beginning with the individual interests, and evolving into group interests and partisan politics, is a masterful synthesis of the need for interest representation (Calhoun 1953, 3-25, 27-44; Spain 1951, 108-17). He also accurately identifies numerical majorities as a conclusive step in the establishment of tyrannical majorities (Calhoun 1953, 27-44). Except for his defense of slavery (40-43), Calhoun perceives the problem of tyrannical majorities as well as anyone.

Finally, Guinier shares in some of Calhoun's views. She demonstrates an appreciation for individual and group interest representation, as Calhoun does. However, she is more focused on the political causes of majoritarian tyranny than the social. Her observation of winner-take-all districting as a primary source of majoritarian tyranny is as important a finding in the conceptualization of the tyranny of the majority as any.

From these four authors I have synthesized two social and three political causes of the tyranny of the majority. The two social causes of the tyranny of the majority are the pursuit of individual and group interests. I believe that these two causes of majoritarian tyranny are sufficient in themselves. Madison, Tocqueville, Calhoun, and Guinier connect both of these causes to majority tyranny.

The three political causes of the tyranny of the majority (the two-party system, winner-take-all districting, and the voting system) are secondary but still important causes. Calhoun and Guinier are primarily responsible for these three being selected. They both had the benefit of history and personal experience to teach them how tyrannical majorities can reveal themselves. Like Madison before them, they found faults in the system that require correction. At the end of this chapter those corrections will be offered. What is offered next is the synthesis of the definition of tyranny.

A Synthesis of the Definition of Tyranny

The definition of the tyranny of the majority begins with Madison's definition of tyranny. He defines tyranny in this way: "The accumulation of all powers, legislative, executive, and judiciary, in the same hands, whether of one, a few, or many, and whether hereditary, self-appointed, or elective, may justly be pronounced the very definition of tyranny" (1961, *Federalist 47*:301).

Dahl interprets Madison's explicit definition of tyranny to mean that "'tyranny' is every severe deprivation of a natural right" (1956, 6). Dahl derives his interpretation of Madison's definition from the idea that what Madison was attempting to say, was that, "the accumulation of all powers in the same hands would lead to severe deprivations of natural rights and hence to tyranny" (Dahl 1956, 6).

I concur with Dahl that Madison's definition meant that "'tyranny' is every severe deprivation of a natural right" (6). The definition at this point is a combination of Madison and Dahl's interpretation of Madison. However, Dahl criticizes Madison for not defining natural rights clearly enough. Dahl is correct, but it is my contention that Madison did not define natural rights because he understood it was the responsibilities of the people to claim what their rights are (Declaration of Independence; Morgan 1988, 131-59).

What this added to the definition of tyranny is that the people determine natural rights. Since it is my assessment that Madison believed that rights had to be determined by the people, I will include my name among those who have helped to form the definition. Therefore, the definition from Madison, Dahl, and Beahm came to be that "tyranny is every severe deprivation of a natural right, as determined to be a natural right by the people."

Although Madison did end up writing most of the Bill of Rights, he did so reluctantly. His decision to write them was finally motivated by his desire to squelch Anti-Federalist complaints that the Constitution did not protect rights adequately (Morgan 1988, 131). Also, he wanted to include rights where there was "no serious objection" and they would be approved by "two-thirds of both houses" and "three-fourths of the state legislatures" (Madison 1977, 12:199). This position by Madison added to the definition that there could be "no serious objection" to natural rights that were being claimed in the Bill of Rights, or elsewhere. By this modification the definition by Madison, Dahl, and Beahm came to be that "Tyranny is every severe deprivation of a natural right, as determined to be a natural right by the people, with no serious objections."

In addition to the definition of tyranny as it stands now, Fishkin contributes the point that "a severe deprivation is the destruction of an essential interest" (Fishkin 1979, 19). Fishkin defines an essential interest as a "private-regarding" want that is essential to one's "life plan." In other words, an essential interest is a natural right. It then follows that the destruction of an essential interest is the destruction of a natural right (1979, 26-32). Fishkin's contribution to the definition of tyranny reveals that "Tyranny is every destruction of a natural right, as determined to be a natural right by the people, with no serious objections."

Roper and Tocqueville contribute a couple of dimensions to the definition of tyranny. Roper contributes that majoritarian tyranny is caused by quantitative factors (political) and qualitative factors (social). Tocqueville identifies a number of quantitative and qualitative elements that contribute to majoritarian tyranny. Elections and legislative powers are two of the quantitative elements that empower majorities (Tocqueville 1969, 2:690-95, 1:248-50). Equality and public opinion are two of the qualitative elements that further majoritarian dominance (Tocqueville 1969, 1:57, 254-56, 2:435-36). Roper and Tocqueville alter the definition of tyranny to mean that "tyranny is every quantitative and qualitative destruction of a natural right, as determined to be a natural right by the people, with no serious objections."

Calhoun uses both quantitative and qualitative elements in his description of tyranny. He believes that the qualitative elements of self-interest, the press, and public opinion encourage the quantitative elements of numerical majorities to wield their influence through suffrage. Calhoun rejects the natural rights approach for the social-compact/community-sanction theory of rights. He believes that all rights are granted by the community (Calhoun 1953, 40-45; Spain 1951, 85-89). Therefore, the use of natural rights in the definition of tyranny had to change to reflect Calhoun's predisposition. The combined definition of tyranny according to Madison, Dahl, Beahm, Fishkin, Roper, Tocqueville, and now Calhoun is that "Tyranny is every quantitative and qualitative destruction of a right, as determined to be a right by the people, with no serious objections."

I decided to remove the words "quantitative" and "qualitative" from the definition, because they were redundant. If tyranny is every destruction of a right, then all quantitative and qualitative rights are included. Quantitative and qualitative elements do provide a perspective from which to understand how majority tyranny manifests itself, but they are not necessary to the definition as long as their contribution is understood. Accordingly, the definition of tyranny now reads "Tyranny is every destruction of a right, as determined to be a right by the people, with no serious objections."

Dahl's contribution to the definition of tyranny has to do with his five criteria necessary to the democratic process. If any one of these five criteria were destroyed, I believe Dahl would find that to be tyrannical. The five criteria that he lists are: equal votes, effective participation, enlightened understanding, final control of the agenda by the *demos*, and inclusiveness (Dahl 1985, 59-60). The five criteria exhibit both quantitative and qualitative elements. I believe, despite the fact that Dahl would disagree with my contention, that the destruction of any one of these could lead to not just tyranny but to tyranny of the majority.

The inclusion of the destruction of Dahl's five criteria necessary to the democratic process did not substantively change the definition of tyranny; it simply added further perspective to the concept of tyranny. Dahl made his greatest substantive contributions to the definition of tyranny when he critiqued Madison's definition in *A Preface to Democratic Theory* (4-33). Consequently, the definition of tyranny remains the same as it was in the last configuration.

Guinier seems to endorse Madison's original definition of tyranny (1994, 3-4). Beyond Madison's definition, Guinier offers two other examples of how tyanny can manifest itself. She finds that winner-take-all districts (quantitative) and a lack of authentic representation for blacks (qualitative) both produce majoritarian tyranny. Winner-take-all districting does not promote the election of representatives who have a minority point of view. The result is that blacks and other minority groups do not receive representation that authentically reflects their views or culture.

Once again, although these new elements add to the understanding of tyranny, they do not change the definition of tyranny. Winner-take-all districting that leads to a lack of authentic representation is the destruction of a right. The definition that I have formulated from Madison, Dahl, Beahm, Fishkin, Roper, Tocqueville, Calhoun, and Guinier is, that "Tyranny is every destruction of a right, as determined to be a right by the people, with no serious objections."

Throughout this study I have claimed that the various definitions of tyranny have also included the definition of tyranny of the majority. I continue to stand by that claim. In this study tyranny has stood for all types of tyranny, from Madison's definition to the final synthesis. It includes the single tyrant, as well as the tyrannical mob.

The contention that "tyranny is every destruction of a right" is perhaps the most controversial clause in the definition. In any form of government, including a democratic republic, people with diverse interests will fall into dispute over their rights. If there is damage to the rights of individuals or groups or a severe deprivation of rights, as Dahl maintains (1956, 6), that is a regrettable situation that should be corrected if at all possible. However, if their rights are destroyed, that is a much more serious affront and can fairly be said to be tyranny. When the destruction of a right occurs, everything that can possibly be done within the realm of the democratic process should be done to correct the violation, including using all checks and balances available.

Admittedly, at times it will be difficult to determine if a severe deprivation or a destruction of a right has occurred. I believe that severe deprivations happen most often when a right is eroded due to a limitation that is put on that right. An example would be when a protester's free speech is limited by being required to stay a certain distance from those he/she is trying to influence, which makes it hard to be heard. A destruction of the right to free speech would exist if the protester was not allowed to be heard at all. A severe deprivation would diminish one's ability to exercise a right; a destruction of a right would eliminate one from exercising it in any meaningful fashion.

The second clause in the definition refers to a right "as determined to be a right by the people." Whether a right is considered to be a natural right, or a sanctioned right, it still has to be identified, sought after, and approved by the people. The right may always have existed a priori, but acknowledgement of its existence and validity is necessary for members of society to enjoy it. The political process is secondary to the acknowledgement of the right by the people, as long as the process fairly allows all voices to be heard. The final clause in the definition recognizes that rights must be determined to be rights by the people, "with no serious objections." A serious objection would be an objection against a right that if approved would cause the destruction of a right for an opposing group. An example would be when a minority or a majority prevents the passage of a constitutional amendment that might damage or destroy their rights. The requirement of supermajorities at both the proposal and ratification stages is evidence of an effort to protect minorities from majoritarian tyranny, within the definition.

The definition of the tyranny of the majority is included in the definition of tyranny because any destruction of a right by a majority is still tyranny. The last two clauses of the definition apply to majoritarian tyranny also, because rights must be determined by the people, with no serious objections. Objections may come from the majority or the minority, but it is important that the majority be prevented from enacting rights that might destroy rights of minority groups. As always, the protection of rights is at the center of preventing tyranny of the majority. This definition works toward that end.

A Synthesis of Rights

Every conception of the tyranny of the majority that supports the notion that it exists is based on the idea that *fundamental rights* of the minority are sometimes harmed by oppressive majorities (Madison 1961, *Federalist 10*:80, 51:323; Tocqueville 1969, 1:238, 1:252; Calhoun 1953, 12-13; Guinier 1994, 3-6). These rights are basically derived from two different sources: natural rights, and social compact or community sanctioned rights (Madison 1961, *Federalist 43*:279; Tocqueville 1969, 1: 239; Calhoun 1953, 43-45; Rossiter 1953, 375-81). Natural rights were derived from, and essentially came to envelop, natural law (Rossiter 1953, 375). Natural law, and thereby natural rights, originated from rights that were thought to exist in the state of nature that have since been carried by civil society into modern times (Hobbes 1962; Locke 1947; Rousseau 1978). Natural law, as it was conceived of in the political theory of the American revolutionary period, was thought to have emanated from three possible sources: divine origin, secularized higher law, and utilitarianism (Rossiter 1953, 366-67). Natural law "formed a system of abstract justice," and marked the "proper sphere of political authority." Most importantly, "natural law was the source of natural rights" (368-69).

Social-compact/community-sanctioned rights were rights that did not pretend to a higher authority than man himself. In representative democracies they were identified by the society at large and were enunciated by the political authority through legislation, or amendments to the constitution. Citizens could also stake a claim to some rights through initiative referendums.

Whatever the source, citizens believe they are justified in claiming rights that they and/or government have identified. Whether these are rights that civil society maintained since humans lived in the state of nature, or were rights fashioned by citizens acting through their political institutions, these rights are of primary importance to the governed. According to proponents of the theory of the tyranny of the majority, these rights apply no less to minorities within democratic republics. Even though Dahl does not believe that majoritarian tyranny exists, he does believe that violating the rights of the minority would violate the precepts of democracy (Dahl 1989, 171-73).

Both Madison's and Tocqueville's conceptions of the tyranny of the majority are based on the natural rights doctrine. Guinier also appears to lean in the direction of basing her conception of majority tyranny on natural rights. Madison believes that there are two methods that may be used to protect the rights of the minority from majoritarian tyranny. The first method requires "creating a will in the community independent of the majority." This method prevails in hereditary or self-appointed governments. The second method relies on there being such diversity in citizens that an "unjust combination" of the majority is unlikely. Madison is convinced that this method would prevail in a "federal republic of the United States." Madison fears that a reliance on the first method would result in a return to the state of nature (1961, 323-24). He states that:

> Justice is the end of government. It is the end of civil society. It ever has been and ever will be pursued until it be obtained, or until liberty be lost in the pursuit. In a society under the forms of which the stronger faction can readily unite and oppress the weaker, anarchy may as truly be said to reign as in a state of nature, where the weaker individual is not secured against the violence of the stronger; and as, in the latter state, even the stronger individuals are prompted, by the uncertainty of their condition, to submit to government which may protect the weak as well as themselves; so, in the former state, will the more powerful factions or parties be gradually induced, by a like motive, to wish for a government which will protect all parties, the weaker as well as the more powerful (Madison 1961, *Federalist 51*:324-25).

Tocqueville, likewise, evokes the need to protect the natural rights of individuals for fear they will be trampled in the stampede of majoritarian desires. He states:

> It is therefore especially necessary in our own democratic age for the true friends of liberty and of human dignity to be on the alert to prevent the social power from lightly sacrificing the private rights of some individuals while carrying through its general designs. At such a time no citizen is so insignificant that he can be trodden down without very dangerous results, and no private rights are of such little importance that they can safely be left subject to arbitrary decisions. There is a simple reason for this: when the private right of an individual is violated at a time when mankind is deeply convinced of the importance and sanctity of such rights, the injury is confined to the person whose right has been infringed. But to infringe such a right now deeply corrupts the mores of the nation and puts the whole of society in danger, because the very idea of this kind of right tends constantly among us to be impaired and lost (Tocqueville 1969, 2:699).

Tocqueville, through inductive reasoning, demonstrates how the harm is first done by the abrogation of individual rights, and then is spread to the general society. He fears that human relations could be reduced to little but power struggles if individual rights are not fully appreciated (Tocqueville 1969, 1:237-40; 2: 699-701: Lamberti 1989, 74). Tocqueville also contends that the right to association is the most natural right that man has, next to acting on his own. The liberty to work in concert with others promotes group interests, as well as individual interests, and Tocqueville finds them to be of almost equal importance (1969, 1:193). Rights are virtue applied to politics, according to Tocqueville. Rights are the representation of justice and good in democratic societies, as citizens are given the lights to see them (1969, 1:237-38).

Guinier asserts that "the fundamental *nature* of the right to vote stems from its role in preserving all other rights." She thinks that the right to vote is made more meaningful by the bond that is created when groups hope to be represented as a united whole. If minority groups are not recognized as a cohesive unit they cannot be adequately represented within the structure of self-government. Their voices can only be heard through their elected representatives. Once a minority group does have a representative in the legislature, it then becomes imperative that his/her voice be equally acknowledged within that institution, in order to make that group's desires felt in the policy-making process (1994, 35-36).

Madison fears a return to the state of nature if minority factions are not well protected (Madison 1961, *Federalist 51*:324-25). Tocqueville fears that the sanctity of rights for all individuals is endangered if the "social power" of the majority pursues its "general designs" at the expense of individual rights (Tocqueville 1969, 2:699). Lani Guinier has identified a similar threat to democracy that has been made apparent by the marginalization of racial minorities in America (Guinier 1994, 103; Raspberry 1998, 5B). She fears that all other rights will be lost for minorities if the right to vote does not translate into meaningful representation for their particular groups. All three of their comments on majoritarian tyranny are in keeping with the state of nature, natural law, and natural rights progression described by Rossiter (1953, 362-81).

Madison, Tocqueville, and Guinier have perceived natural rights, as they evolved from natural law, to stem from divine origin, secularized higher law, and utilitarianism, as Rossiter has suggested (1953, 366-67). I believe that Madison has invoked all three approaches in applying natural rights to his conception of the tyranny of the majority (Madison 1961, *Federalist 37*:227-28; 37:230-31; 1977, 11:297-98; 12:196-99; Morgan 1988, 138; Matthews 1995, 59-63). Tocqueville identifies divine, moral, and political rights as existing, but believes that divine and moral rights have diminished and left political rights standing alone (1969, 1:239). He employs secularized higher law by citing virtue as being integral to rights (1: 237-8). He rests on utilitarianism by connecting rights with personal interests, and then connecting personal interests with association (1: 193). Guinier has taken a utilitarian approach to natural rights by recognizing that all other rights are derived from the "fundamental nature of the right to vote." It is a utilitarian approach because she simply wants minority groups to be fairly represented by their vote (1994, 35-36).

As noted in chapter 2, I believe that Madison didn't define natural rights because he didn't want to leave any out, and he wasn't sure that enumerating rights would protect against majoritarian tyranny. The responsibility for specifying rights was one that should be left to the people, and/or their representatives. In other words, only citizens and/or their representatives had the right to say what their rights are (Madison 1977, 12:196-99; Morgan 1988, 138).

Tocqueville concurs with Madison on how rights are determined. He did not define natural rights because citizens would do it for themselves. He thought that the parameters of the people's rights could only be determined by them. They would know to what extent rights should be exercised, and where the limitations should be set. Citizens would know how to exercise their rights reasonably because they would have had experience doing so. They would not violate the rights of others because they would not want their own violated (1969, 237-40). Tocqueville believed that natural rights issue from natural equality (Zetterbaum 1987, 781).

Since Guinier says little about rights it is hard to know what her sentiments are about them. She clearly thinks that the right to vote is a fundamental right that all other rights depend upon. She does not suggest a theoretical underpinning for why she believes this to be the case. I feel that it would be safe to speculate that she supports the notion that the people can determine what their rights are if they are to be trusted to vote in the first place. The utilitarian approach stemming from the natural rights doctrine (Rossiter 1953, 366-67) suggests that people naturally know what is in their best interest, and they would vote and identify rights based on those interests. Therefore, I place Guinier in the natural rights camp (Guinier 1994, 35-36).

Calhoun and Dahl do not believe in natural rights, but Calhoun does believe that man had a certain nature. According to Calhoun, man's nature was constituted by the Creator with the contradictory purposes of existing as a social being that is primarily self-interested. Government is needed to intervene when these individual interests conflict (Calhoun 1953, 3-7, 43-45; Spain 1951, 43-45).

Dahl rejects the natural/prior rights doctrine (1956, 45) in favor of the rights necessary to the democratic process. Dahl argues that the right to self-government is the most important right of all (1956, 24-26). He concurs with Guinier that voting is an essential ingredient of "political democracy" (1956, 59). Dahl also promotes the maximization of political equality (1956, 63-85; 1996, 639-48).

Differing from Tocqueville, Madison, Guinier, and Dahl, Calhoun does not believe that men are created equal. He holds that men are born with differing talents and abilities, appropriate to their functions in life. He believes that men are created to fit their conditions. The Creator has also supplied different social and political states to fit the various conditions of man (Calhoun 1953, 7).

Calhoun believes that we are all born into the subjugation of those who are already here. However, some are more subjugated than others. Slaves were born into the social and political state that fit their talents and abilities. Limiting the rights of blacks was allowable in Calhoun's way of thinking, because citizens determine through their government who shall have rights in a democratic republic. Calhoun argues that rights had always been granted through governmental authority, because no other authority existed that could do so (Calhoun 1953, 43-45; Spain 1951, 85-91).

While Calhoun was clearly using his argument for government-granted rights as a thinly disguised veil for upholding slavery, his point that citizens determine rights through their government is not much different from what Madison, Tocqueville, and Guinier come to by way of the natural rights argument. Calhoun's method of understanding rights has the supreme irony of being applied equally to his complaint that southerners were being tyrannized by the North, while slaves were simply living in a condition that fit them. Calhoun believed that self-interest could cause men to use tyrannical majorities to promote their interests; it is indeed tragic that Calhoun could not see the tyrant in himself.

Madison should not escape the wrath of those of us who criticize Calhoun for attempting to defend slavery. Madison's relative silence in comparison to Calhoun on the issue of slavery should not acquit him of the same wrong. Perhaps Madison deserves worse, since the natural rights doctrine requires protection of everyone's rights. Calhoun was being logically consistent in his construction of rights, but immoral. Tocqueville condemns slavery, and finds it to be a possible source of revolution in the future (Tocqueville 1969, 317-20; 639).

Beyond Madison and Calhoun sharing some cognitive dissonance on the issue of slavery, Madison, Tocqueville, and Guinier do share at least one view on the issue of rights with Calhoun and Dahl. Madison, Tocqueville, and Guinier support the concept of social-compact/community-sanctioned rights, as do Calhoun and Dahl. Madison, Tocqueville, and Guinier never discount the idea that citizens act through their government to identify and bestow rights. Where they do differ with Calhoun and Dahl is in their assertions of natural rights. Madison, Tocqueville, and probably Guinier accept that certain rights have always existed, waiting only to be fully recognized. Social-compact/community-sanctioned rights may be little more than natural rights completely realized. Yet, there is one important distinction between natural rights and social-compact/community sanctioned-rights.

Calhoun, paradoxically, believes that man has a nature that forecasts what his social and political state will be, but he does not accept that the same Creator that gave man a nature also gave him natural rights. The distinction is an important one when it comes to how slaves will live, and it is also important when evaluating how rights affect one's perception of the tyranny of the majority. In the case of Calhoun and his rejection of natural rights, doing so meant the exclusion of blacks from a number of rights. Therein lies the one clear advantage that natural rights have over social-compact/community-sanctioned rights: natural rights are more inclusive.

It is my contention that natural rights are intended for all people within a given society. Social-compact/community-sanctioned rights may or may not apply to all people in a society, as in Calhoun's interpretation. One might reasonably argue that Madison fared no better with his interpretation of natural rights regarding slavery, but his actions were inconsistent with the natural rights doctrine. In other words, Madison failed to live up to his own theoretical position. Calhoun's upholding of slavery is not necessarily inconsistent with the social-compact/community-sanctioned rights approach.

If some people are left out of the bargain in the claiming of rights, they are being ostracized from the society at some level. While any method of deriving rights can be used as an argument to deprive certain segments of the society of their rights, the natural rights doctrine leans more in the direction of encouraging the claiming of rights by individuals and groups, and the honoring of those rights by the government, than other methods. It does so by acknowledging that those rights have always existed.

The evidence of this inclusion can be found in various amendments to the Constitution. The Thirteenth, Fourteenth, Fifteenth, Nineteenth, and Twenty-Sixth Amendments have all been added to extend rights to people of our society who had not been made full citizens. The extension of rights in America was well summarized by Tocqueville in his statement that "in America the people were invested with political rights at a time when it was difficult for them to make ill use of them because the citizens were few and their mores simple. As they have grown more powerful, the Americans have not appreciably increased the powers of democracy; rather they have extended its domain" (1969, 239).

Extending rights is paramount to prevention of majoritarian tyranny. Central to any synthesis of the concepts of the tyranny of the majority is the need to understand how rights underlie the concept. The natural rights doctrine is more conducive to the conceptualization of a theory of the tyranny of the majority for two reasons.

First, I believe that the natural rights approach is more inclusive, and inclusiveness is vital to the development of any conception of a theory of the tyranny of the majority. Since anyone might find himself a part of a minority at some time, it is important to protect his rights as well as the majority is protected. Protecting minority rights is an essential ingredient in the democratic process (Dahl 1989, 169-73). The natural rights approach does a better job of protecting the process because it is more inclusive.

Second, I find that the natural rights approach covers most of what the social-compact/community-sanction approach does. As previously mentioned, social-compact/community-sanctioned rights can be seen as the uncovering of natural rights. Rights must be sanctioned somewhere, at some time, in order to be claimed and protected. The declaring of rights may happen in a number of ways, including constitutional amendment, conventions (state or federal), initiatives, or through the legislative process. Whatever the method, the social-compact/community-sanction identification of rights comes into play at some level, so that rights are acknowledged and formalized. The identifying of rights through the social compact/community sanction method is the recognition that natural rights have existed since humans dwelt in the state of nature.

It is my conclusion that the natural rights approach to understanding and applying rights is superior to the social-compact/community-sanction approach, for the previously stated reasons. The approach that is taken to facilitate rights often sets the parameters of what corrections are taken to alleviate majoritarian tyranny. The natural rights doctrine is more inclusive as to who can claim rights, and how they may go about doing so. In making corrections to the tyranny of the majority, the more inclusive the approach to rights, the more possible solutions to the dilemma of the tyranny of the majority.

A Synthesis of the Corrections to the Tyranny of the Majority

The corrections to the tyranny of the majority are many and varied. For Madison the corrections take the form of constitutional checks and balances. These checks and balances are necessary to control the effects of majority faction when the republican principle of majority rule is not able to do so. The government, particularly the legislature, is also capable of developing tyrannical majorities. Therefore, checks and balances may be required to prevent one branch from tyrannizing the others, and to prevent government from tyrannizing the people generally (Madison 1961, *Federalist 51:*320-25; 10:77-84).

The separation of powers, as set out in the U.S. Constitution, grants particular powers to the three branches. It also divides the legislature into two houses. A further step of dividing the government between state and federal levels is made to prevent citizens from being tyrannized by an overly centralized government. The separation of powers was also meant to prevent tyrannizing majorities from dominating the government and the people (Madison *1961, Federalist 51:*320-25).

Tocqueville detects six ways that majoritarian tyranny can be tempered: the existence of free political association; a related freedom of civil association; the existence of newspapers and their ability to facilitate association; the absence of administrative centralization; the counterbalancing affect of the American legal profession; and the jury as a political institution. Tocqueville believes that associations encourage individuals to join forces against majority tyranny, and that newspapers help them to do that. He also believes that lawyers act to slow down unbridled democracy, with their aristocratic distrust of "the ill considered passions of democracy" (1969, 1:264). Juries engage the populace in the political process. This places them in the position of having to judge their fellow men. From this they learn how they might be judged and they come to understand more about citizen equity. Juries help to shape the nation's judgement (1969, 1: 189-95, 2:520-24, 2:513-17, 2:517-20, 1:89-92, 1:262-63, 1:262-76).

Calhoun and Guinier share the view that interest representation is necessary to avoiding majoritarian tyranny. Calhoun maintains that concurrent majorities, which would represent minority interests, would stifle numerical majorities that turn into tyrannical majorities (1953, 27-31). Guinier argues that interest representation is the only fair way to make sure that minority groups are fully represented. She suggests that cumulative voting will promote interest representation, and bring an end to winner-take-all districting that prevents minorities from receiving authentic representation (1994, 94-98, 117-18, 14-16, 119, 123, 137, 55-58).

Guinier also recommends that interest representation can be achieved through several different forms of proportional representation, one of which is cumulative voting. The other alternatives are the party listing system, where parties are granted seats in proportion to the percentage of votes they win, and the preference voting system, where voters simply rank candidates in the order they prefer them (1998, 258-59). She expresses favor for the "mixed system now used in Germany" (1998, 269).

I also endorse the mixed system of proportional representation used in Germany, but any reasonable form of proportional representation system would be an improvement over the present winner-take-all system used in America. The addition of the semiproportional representation system of cumulative voting, while a worthwhile method of proportional representation, does not produce the results for minorities that the party listing system or the preference voting system would be apt to. I believe that the party listing system, the preference voting system, or some mix of these, along with cumulative voting, would provide a proportional representation system that would be most suited to correcting the three main political causes of majority tyranny (those causes being the two-party system, winner-take-all districting, and the voting system). A proportional representation (PR) system (particularly the party listing system) would most likely moderate the two-party system in America, by providing greatly enhanced opportunities to elect minority party candidates in numbers equal to the votes they receive. A PR system would also make great strides toward moderating or eliminating the winner-take-all districting that now results in so many voters wasting their votes.

Lastly, a PR system would moderate two of the three problems with the voting system, depending on its construction. It could minimize or eliminate single-member districting, which would bring about a more equitable reflection of minority sentiments. It could also remove winner-take-all voting. However, it would not take away the single-day (Tuesday) voting problem. Nevertheless, if a PR system were to replace the present system of voting and representation in the United States, I think the chance of changing the voting day would be greatly enhanced.

Although I believe that the political causes of majority tyranny may be mostly eliminated by changes in the democratic process, the two main social causes cannot be prevented from initially occurring. The effects of individual and group interests that lead to the development of tyrannical majorities may be moderated or corrected at the political level by the use of some or all of the methods available to do so, but they can never be stopped from coming into existence. Madison was correct about majority factions that cannot be checked by other factions; the government itself must halt their heated passions. Therefore, tyranny of the majority will continue to be caused by individual and group interests, and will need to be corrected for at the political level.

The alternative corrections to the tyranny of the majority can also be classified as quantitative (political) or qualitative (social) (Roper 1989, 17). Examples of quantitative corrections would be checks and balances, the separation of powers, political associations, the absence of administrative centralization, juries, concurrent majorities, cumulative voting, and other systems of proportional representation. Examples of qualitative checks would be factions, civic associations, lawyers, and newspapers (the media generally). The problem with qualitative checks is that they are often ineffective and have to be supported by quantitative checks.

In the final analysis I contend that the social causes of majority tyranny cannot be prevented. Social checks may serve the purpose of deterring some minor threats from individual and group interests, but they are not powerful enough to prevent majoritarian tyranny from occurring. Political checks can't prevent the occurrence of majority tyranny from social causes either, but political checks are a far more powerful force in containing social causes once they have reared their heads.

Conclusion

It is my position that majority tyranny is caused by individual interests, group interests, the two-party system, winner-take-all districting, and the voting system in America. The two root causes of majority tyranny are the social elements of individual and group interests. The three remaining political causes of tyrannical majorities are secondary causes, but still important ones.

I also hold that the definition of tyranny, and thereby the tyranny of the majority, to be that "Tyranny is every destruction of a right, as determined to be a right by the people, with no serious objections."

This definition includes the tyranny of the majority, because rights are destroyed by it. Also, the rights to be protected must be determined by the people, with no serious objections. This means that majorities and minorities determine what rights will be protected.

Of the two distinct theoretical conceptions of rights, natural rights and community-sanctioned rights, I believe natural rights to be more conducive to the conceptualization of a theory of the tyranny of the majority. I believe this because the natural rights approach is more inclusive, and inclusiveness is important if minorities are to be protected. Also, I submit that the community-sanction approach to rights is mostly covered by the natural rights approach. The community-sanction approach is mostly about recognizing and formalizing natural rights.

The way that rights are protected often has to do with how the tyranny of the majority is corrected. Qualitative, or social corrections, are less effective in stopping tyranny of the majority than quantitative, or political corrections. While the social causes of majority tyranny, individual and group interests, cannot be prevented from occurring, the three political causes—the two-party system, winner-take-all districting, and the voting system—may be prevented from occurring if a proportional representation system is used to replace the present system in America.

What I have provided through this study is a clarification of the conceptualizations of the tyranny of the majority from five different authors, on four different points. Madison, Tocqueville, Calhoun, Dahl, and Guinier have been examined regarding their conceptualizations of the tyranny of the majority, their definition of tyranny, their perception of rights, and their corrections to the tyranny of the majority. I have done this with the intent of shedding new light on these four points, and thereby extending the literature on the subject of the tyranny of the majority. I have also synthesized the authors' perspectives on the four main points.

From the synthesis of the four main points I have identified and categorized the five main causes, two of which are root causes, of the tyranny of the majority. I have reconstructed a new definition of tyranny, as it relates to the tyranny of the majority. I also have identified and explained why natural rights are more conducive to the conceptualization of theories of the tyranny of the majority. Furthermore, I have suggested that the three main political causes of majoritarian tyranny can be largely prevented by the acceptance of some form of proportional representation. However, the social causes, individual and group interests, cannot be prevented, only contained by political correctives.

I maintain that the tyranny of the majority will continue to be a pock on the governing process in America, if nothing is done to encourage the installment of a proportional representation system. If nothing is done, constitutional checks will have to be increasingly used to protect minority interests, to the dissatisfaction of both majorities and minorities. Most of the Western industrialized democracies have some form of proportional representation system. I believe the United States would be well served by following their example.

References

Calhoun, John C. 1953. *A Disquisition on Government and Selections on the Discourse*. New York: Liberal Arts Press.

Dahl, Robert A. 1989. *Democracy and Its Critics*. New Haven, Conn.: Yale University Press.

———. 1956. *A Preface to Democratic Theory*. Chicago: University of Chicago Press.

———. 1985. *A Preface to Economic Democracy*. Berkeley: Universtiy of California Press.

Fishkin, James S. 1979. *Tyranny and Legitimacy: A Critique of Political Theories*. Baltimore: Johns Hopkins University Press.

Guinier, Lani. 1994. *The Tyranny of the Majority: Fundamental Fairness in Representative Democracy*. Foreword by Stephen L. Carter. New York: The Free Press.

Hobbes, Thomas. 1962. *Leviathan*. Ed. Michael Oakeshott. Introduction by Richard S. Peters. New York: Collier Books.

Lamberti, Jean-Claude. 1989. *Tocqueville and the Two Democracies*. Translated by Arthur Goldhammer. Cambridge, Mass.: Harvard University Press.

Locke, John. 1947. *Two Treatises of Government*. With a Supplement: *Patriarcha*. Ed. and introduction by Thomas I. Cook. New York: Hafner Press.

Madison, James. 1977. *The Papers of James Madison*. Ed. By Robert A. Rutland, Charles F. Hobson, William M.E. Rachal, and Jeanne K. Sisson. Fifteen volumes to date. Charlottesville: University Press of Virginia.

————. With Alexander Hamilton, and John Jay. 1961. *The Federalist Papers*. Introduction by Clinton Rossiter. New York: New American Library.

Matthews, Richard. K. 1995. *If Men Were Angels: James Madison and the Heartless Empire of Reason*. Lawrence: University Press of Kansas.

Morgan, Robert J. 1988. *James Madison on the Constitution and the Bill of Rights*. Contributions in Legal Studies, No. 48. New York: Greenwood Press.

Raspberry, William. "'Quota Queen' Guinier Has Something Important to Say About Our Troubles." *Lincoln Journal-Star*. May 18, 1998. 5B.

Roper, Jon. 1989. *Democracy and Its Critics: Anglo-American Democratic Thought in the Nineteenth Century*. London: Unwin Hyman.

Rossiter, Clinton. 1953. *Seedtime of the Republic: The Origin of the American Tradition of Political Liberty*. New York: Harcourt, Brace.

Rousseau, Jean-Jacques. 1978. *On The Social Contract: With Geneva Manuscript and Political Economy*. Ed. Roger D. Masters. Trans. by Judith R. Masters. New York: St. Martin's Press.

Spain, August D. 1951. *The Political Theory of John C. Calhoun*. New York: Bookman Associates.

Tocqueville, Alexis de. 1969. *Democracy in America*. Trans. George Lawrence. Ed. J. P. Mayer. New York: Harper and Row.

Zetterbaum, Marvin. 1987. "Alexis de Tocqueville." *History of Political Philosophy*. 3rd. ed. Ed. Leo Strauss and Joseph Cropsey. Chicago: University of Chicago Press.

Index

views of, 68; relationship to natural
rights, 96, 97, 100; source of, 92
compromise: Calhoun's views of, 59
concurrent majorities, 6, 7, 46, 58–59,
98
Congress: electoral checks, 23–24;
external checks, 24; internal checks,
23; separation of powers, 22, 23.
See also legislatures
constitutional checks: Dahl's views of,
71–72, 80.70; Madison's views of,
98
Constitutional Convention: Madison
and, 11, 19, 24, 25; natural law
concept and, 19
constitutional majorities, 7, 58–59. *See
also* concurrent majorities
constitutions: Calhoun's views of, 56
Constitution, U.S.: Madison and, 11,
24, 25; natural rights and, 97;
nullification movement and, 45;
separation of powers, 22, 98. *See
also* Bill of Rights
cumulative voting, 6, 77, 78–79, 85, 98,
99

Dahl, Robert A.: corrections to tyranny
of the majority, 7, 70–72; criteria
for democratic process, 66–67, 90;
Guinier's views of tyranny of the
majority and, 80–81; influence of,
61; on Madison, 21; Madisonian
definition of tyranny and, 13, 15,
65–66, 89; *The Political Thought of
the American Revolution,* 13; *A
Preface to Democratic Theory,* 13,
61, 64, 66, 90; on proportional
representation, 80; views of rights,
67–70, 95; views of social checks,
70–71, 85–86; views of tyranny,
65–67; views of tyranny of the
majority, 6, 62–65; violation of
minority rights and, 92; *Who
Governs?,* 72.
Declaration of Independence: natural
rights and, 13, 14–15
democracy: majority rule and, 1
Democracy in America (Tocqueville),
87–88

Democratic Party: preference voting
and, 78
democratic process: constitutional
checks and, 70; Dahl's criteria for,
66–67, 90; prior rights and, 67–68
Dennis v. United States, 3
districting: race-based, 74–75. *See also*
winner-take-all districts
divine rights, 34

elections: majorities and, 89;
Tocqueville on, 32. *See also*
presidential elections; suffrage
electoral checks, 23–24
Electoral College, 24
equality: Dahl's views of, 61, 64, 72;
maximization of, 64; need for
associations and, 39; public opinion
and, 30–33; Tocqueville's views of,
30–33, 36, 84, 87–88; tyranny of
the majority and, 30–33, 84, 87–88,
89–90
Espionage Act (1917), 3
essential interests, 15–16, 89
establishment clause, 3
executive branch: checks and balances,
24

factions: controlling the effects of, 21–
25; group interests and, 86;
Madison's views of, 12, 21–25, 84,
86, 87; tyranny of the majority and,
12, 84, 86, 87, 99
federalism: corrections to tyranny of
the majority, 22–23; Tocqueville's
views of, 42
Federalist Papers, 1, 13, 22
filibustering, 23
First Amendment rights, 3–4
Fishkin, James S., 14, 15–16, 66, 89
freedom of assembly: political
associations and, 37–38
free speech: tyranny of the majority
and, 3

Germany: mixed system of
representation, 79, 99
Golden Rule, 17–18

About the Author

Dr. Beahm received his B.S. in political science from Black Hills State University in Spearfish, South Dakota. He received his M.A. and Ph.D. in political science from the University of Nebraska, Lincoln. He has taught at Doane College in Lincoln and Crete, Nebraska. Currently he teaches and does research in the areas of political thought, constitutional law, and American politics as an assistant professor of political science at Dowling College in Oakdale, Long Island, New York.